Making Schools Work

Joseph L. DeVitis & Linda Irwin-DeVitis
General Editors

Vol. 8

PETER LANG
New York • Washington, D.C./Baltimore • Bern
Frankfurt am Main • Berlin • Brussels • Vienna • Oxford

Carolyn R. Hodges and Olga M. Welch

Montante Family Library
D'Youville College

MAKING SCHOOLS WORK

Negotiating Educational Meaning and Transforming the Margins

PETER LANG
New York • Washington, D.C./Baltimore • Bern
Frankfurt am Main • Berlin • Brussels • Vienna • Oxford

Library of Congress Cataloging-in-Publication Data

Hodges, Carolyn R.
Making schools work: negotiating educational meaning
and transforming the margins / Carolyn R. Hodges and Olga M. Welch.
p. cm. — (Adolescent cultures, school, and society; v. 8)
Includes bibliographical references (p.).
1. Compensatory education—United States—Longitudinal studies. 2. Academic
achievement—United States—Longitudinal studies. 3. Children
with social disabilities—Education (Secondary)—United States—Longitudinal studies.
4. African American high school students—Longitudinal studies.
5. Identity (Psychology). I. Welch, Olga M. II. Title.
III. Adolescent cultures, school and society; v. 8.
LC213.2 .H63   370.11′1—dc21   2002018986
ISBN 0-8204-3981-9
ISSN 1091-1464

Die Deutsche Bibliothek-CIP-Einheitsaufnahme

Hodges, Carolyn R.:
Making schools work: negotiating educational meaning
and transforming the margins / Carolyn R. Hodges and Olga M. Welch.
–New York; Washington, D.C./Baltimore; Bern;
Frankfurt am Main; Berlin; Brussels; Vienna; Oxford: Lang.
(Adolescent cultures, school, and society; Vol. 8)
ISBN 0-8204-3981-9

Cover design by Dutton & Sherman

The paper in this book meets the guidelines for permanence and durability
of the Committee on Production Guidelines for Book Longevity
of the Council of Library Resources.

© 2003 Peter Lang Publishing, Inc., New York
275 Seventh Avenue, 28th Floor, New York, NY 10001
www.peterlangusa.com

All rights reserved.
Reprint or reproduction, even partially, in all forms such as microfilm,
xerography, microfiche, microcard, and offset strictly prohibited.

Printed in the United States of America

_C 213.2
. H 63
2003

TABLE OF CONTENTS

APR 19 2004

ACKNOWLEDGMENTS

The findings offered in this work represent an additional dimension to the longitudinal study on academic achievement and identity construction on which we reported in our earlier book, *Standing Outside on the Inside: Black Adolescents and the Construction of Academic Identity* (SUNY 1997).* Numerous colleagues, students, university and project staff, and family and friends supported and contributed to this long-term project by offering constructive advice and criticism, providing funding, facilitating meetings with school officials, and—perhaps most important of all—listening to and encouraging us throughout the process.

Funding provided by the University of Tennessee made it possible for us to secure partial released time from teaching, to travel to conferences to present our research, to sponsor academic and career counseling workshops for Project EXCEL students, and to maintain a Project EXCEL office and secretarial support. Particularly helpful in this regard was John Peters, former Vice-Chancellor for Academic Affairs, who was instrumental in our obtaining financial support for the duration of this phase of the project. We are indebted to the former deans of our colleges, Glennon Rowell of Education and Lorayne Lester of Arts and Sciences, who enthusiastically endorsed the cross-disciplinary value of our research, and to the members of the Project EXCEL Advisory Board, made up of educational, business, and civic leaders who served as an invaluable link to the community.

For assisting us with instruction, academic counseling, and weekend workshops to improve reading, writing, and testing skills we are extremely grateful to high school teachers, university faculty, and graduate students who taught classes and led workshops. Several school counselors aided our work by providing essential records and data. Special thanks are due to the directors of the Beck Cultural Center, where space was provided for special weekend sessions with Project EXCEL students.

No book can be completed without dependable and skilled secretarial support. We cannot offer enough thanks to Ann Galloway, who staffed the Project EXCEL office and worked on various stages of the manuscript, and to Linda Green, who prepared the final version for publication. Their careful attention to detail, patience, and genuine interest in our endeavors were invaluable to the successful conclusion of this study. Special recognition must be extended to our hard-working production editor, Lisa Dillon, and to the series editors, Joseph DeVitis and Linda Irwin-DeVitis who recognized the value of our research as a part of their series.

Of course, no amount of gratitude can completely express the importance of those who stand at the center of this work—the students and their parents. Their challenges and triumphs comprise the impulse for and core of our work and, it is hoped, will inspire new studies committed to making schools work and compelling students to excel.

* "Reprinted by permission from *Standing Outside on the Inside: Black Adolescents and the Construction of Academic Identity* by Olga M. Welch and Carolyn R. Hodges, the State University of New York Press. ©1997 State University of New York. All Rights Reserved."

INTRODUCTION
Unmasking the Culture of Schooling for African American Adolescents

> When one talks about marginality and otherness one must always ask, marginal to what? other to whom?
>
> —R. Ferguson

As Ferguson (1993) reminds us, questions about marginality and otherness are difficult to answer, since "the place where power is exercised is often a hidden place" (p. 9). Moreover, the margins are not only sites of oppression but, for some, may be points of resistance as well (hooks, 1994). Thus, in the examination of issues related to marginality and representation of self with respect to adolescents and schooling, Wexler suggests that a process exists that shapes the distribution of identity. This process involves a kind of tracking system in schools in which single behaviors, words, or other kinds of signs are accepted as representations of self. As a result, "standards or values and the social instruments to achieve them are established which, in turn, govern the interactional resources employed by students in their accomplishment" (Wexler, 1992, p. 9). If the experiences of marginality, otherness, and their relationship to the "mythical norm" (Lorde, 1984) in education are to be better understood, then an examination of the social and cultural relations as well as representations of self that occur in school settings must be conducted. Understanding how educationally disadvantaged adolescents—comprised predominantly but not exclusively of African Americans—who had the potential to attend college defined themselves as "scholars" and the possible relationship of such a definition to their achievement became the focus of our nine-year longitudinal study. By educationally disadvantaged, we mean those students who had the potential and the desire to attend college, but for whom performance and educational background proved obstacles. Like Ferguson (1993), we believe that identity development for educationally disadvantaged adolescents, particularly those of color, involves issues of marginality and otherness that must be explored if appropriate academic interventions are to be developed. Indeed, other researchers have examined complex issues of identity construction within students who, whether based on race, gender, class, or ableness, define themselves or are defined as being in the margins of school life (Apple, 1990; Cross, 1991; Hall, 1992; Hudak, 1993; McCarthy, 1990). However, we chose to situate our work within a construct, i.e., scholar identity, which emerged in our own academic development.

As two African American female professors at a large research institution, who had been identified early as college material, we found that our ability to succeed academically, even in the face of systemic racial and gender barriers, involved the development of a "scholar identity." This scholar identity, which we both traced to adolescence, evolved as a series of negotiations and reconstructions of our identities that we used to counteract stereotypic messages of Black intellectual inferiority and the consequent limited career and educational options. The powerful nature of the scholar self in our own academic lives became the catalyst for the nine-year investigation of the relationship between academic achievement and identity construction presented in our book *Standing Outside on the Inside: Black Adolescents and the Construction of Academic Identity* (Welch & Hodges 1997). Our study placed academic achievement at its center and used McClelland's seminal definition of achievement motivation as a point of departure. McClelland's definition suggests that achievement motivation exists as a "stable personality trait possessed only by those individuals whose culture (including race, environment, child-rearing practices, religious values, and social class) stress competition with standards of excellence" (McClelland 1953 as cited in Castenell, 1984, p. 436). For us, this definition fails to account for individuals who succeeded academically despite disadvantaged backgrounds. It also implies that achievement motivation cannot be cultivated in some populations, even if academic enrichment is provided, and thereby calls into question the premise that such enrichment can significantly improve post-secondary admissions for educationally disadvantaged African American adolescents.

Working with three small cohorts (10–13 students) of primarily, though not exclusively, African American adolescents in two high schools, we conducted our study of the relationship between pre-college enrichment experiences and the development of academic ethos (scholar identity), first in a summer school/university enrichment program we designed and later as part of the college preparatory curriculum in the center city school from which most of the study participants were drawn. The study, Project EXCEL (Encouraging Excellence in Children Extends Learning), examined the development of scholar identity in juniors (first cohort) and sophomores (second and third cohorts) who identified themselves and were identified as college bound by teachers and guidance counselors. The first cohort consisted of rising juniors who participated in a university-sponsored enrichment program that emphasized reading, writing, and foreign language study (either German or French). Based on the findings from the pilot study with the first cohort, both the second and third cohorts were composed of rising sophomores. Because of the three fold emphasis on reading, writing, and foreign language study, the program had cross-disciplinary implications, since admission to and persistence in college are related to the ability to read and write and because proficiency in a foreign language has been proven to increase literacy in the native language. In designing the study, our questions were:

1. Can a transition program build academic ethos (scholar identity) in educationally disadvantaged African American and European American college-bound students? and
2. What combination of subjects and classroom experiences are most critical to the development of academic ethos?

The focus on these questions represented our hypothesis that, in addition to potential and appropriate pre-college preparation, educationally disadvantaged adolescents had to develop their own definitions of scholarship in order to achieve academically. Even with White adolescents who presumably enjoy White Privilege (McIntosh, 1992), development of definitions of scholarship could not be assumed to emerge and to be uniform. Rather, if they emerged, they had to represent the students' personally constructed commitments to and definitions of excellence. This development of self-constructed definitions of the scholar that evolves as a result of academic study became central to all of the goals in Project EXCEL. Moreover, in exploring this concept of scholar identity, we chose to concentrate on students who did not represent those with the highest academic qualifications. Instead, the participants in all three cohorts were those students who expressed a desire to attend college and who exhibited academic promise but who did not always achieve the grade point averages or standardized test scores generally used as strong predictors of college success. Nor were all of these students economically disadvantaged. Some were the children of college graduates, while others had parents and/or relatives who held clerical jobs, worked in construction, or held entry-level managerial positions. Our decision to work with these students was not accidental. Rather, it represented the opportunity to test our tacit theory that the development of an identity grounded in scholarship required, in addition to course work, role modeling, and study skills, the student's ownership of his/her construction of scholarship and evolution as a scholar. This meant that in addition to potential and appropriate pre-college preparation, educationally disadvantaged African American adolescents had to develop a personal commitment to excellence that emerged as they engaged in challenging intellectual tasks and career goal-setting. We refer to this commitment as scholar ethos—that is, an academic identity that promotes achievement based on a recognition that exclusion from educational opportunities may be unrelated to either potential or performance. As Edwards and Polite (1992) note:

> A belief in choices has always fueled black ambition, for even in the face of limited opportunities, one remains free to choose—to choose excellence over mediocrity, for instance, or character over vanity, or work and struggle over idle irresponsibility. These are the choices too that go against stereotype and make for one being "a credit to the race" (p. 137).

To go against the stereotype for EXCEL students meant building this identity by intentionally engaging in individual explorations of the meaning of scholar and scholarship in concert with an academic program of study that sought to provide the skills in reading, writing, and foreign language study needed to succeed in college regardless of the major chosen. In designing the course of study in EXCEL, deliberate attention was given to these literacy components rather than to equally important math, science, or computer studies because of their cross-curriculum application, for to matriculate successfully in a post-secondary institution, students must possess the ability to articulate their ideas in both oral and written communication in a wide variety of courses.

We believed that EXCEL students, armed with these skills and their individually crafted definitions of scholarship of themselves as scholars, might undertake the "border crossing" activities advocated by Giroux (1992), for instance, such as the ability to use formal or informal English, depending on the conversational context and the behavioral expectations attached. This border crossing makes explicit for students the culture of power that members of marginalized groups must understand if they are to integrate with mainstream culture without relinquishing their own cultures (Collins, 1993). The term "culture of power" is used to draw attention to the premise that certain ways of self-representation, of talking, interacting, and writing, for example, can serve to facilitate or hinder an individual's chances for success within mainstream institutions. When an institution is dominated by individuals from the majority culture, facility with that culture, the culture of power, can contribute to a minority person's chances for success. Often the culture-of-home advocates' failure to acknowledge the importance of minority students' access to the culture of power leads to minority parents' resistance to a curriculum and instruction that promotes, exclusively, the culture of the home. Success in institutions—schools, workplaces, and so on—is predicated upon acquisition of the culture of those who are in power. Children from middle-class homes tend to do better in school than those from non-middle-class homes because the culture of school is based on the culture of the upper and middle classes of those in power (Delpit, 1995, p. 25).

Inherent in our own development of scholar ethos was an understanding of schools and schooling that made explicit the culture of power described by Collins (1993) and Delpit (1995). Thus, with EXCEL students we viewed the construction of their own scholar identities as a possible counterbalance to the negative messages of Black intellectual inferiority that they might encounter. We further conjectured that, depending on its use, scholar identity might likewise become a mechanism of student agency, since to be Black and a success in America is largely viewed as an exception—a departure from the rule, an aberration. It is a view that skews black ambition and blinds white perception, for it is a vision still clouded in the pathology of race. Race perhaps more significantly also shapes expectations and assumptions—what we think we can and cannot be. And it is very often low expectations—black ability, for black possibility—that both limits and drives black ambition (Edwards & Polite, 1992, pp. 132–33).

Thus, some EXCEL students undertook academic work from which evolved a personalized construction of scholarship; their interviews (while they participated in the program and during the first year after graduation) suggested a belief that relinquishing their cultural self was unnecessary for successful matriculation in schools. Nor did they identify a conflict between the academic self and cultural self termed "acting white," suggested in a study by Fordham and Ogbu (1986). Instead, our findings indicate that in concert with an increased and individual efficacy in reading, writing, and foreign language, for some EXCEL students, the scholar identity became part of an oppositional identity (Cross, 1991), which they used to confront messages of academic inferiority and/or racial discrimination.

In the first book, we described the research design, questions, and findings related to scholar identity and achievement motivation with the first two cohorts of Project EXCEL students. In this text, we focus on findings from the third cohort of EXCEL students from Augustana High School. Students from the first two cohorts were taken from two high schools (Ryan and Augustana, a medium sized city (250,000) in the southeast region), the first with a "mixed" population (60% African American, 40% European American) and the second with a 98% African American population. By the time the second cohort had finished high school, Ryan High School had been closed by the city and the students dispersed to other area high schools. With the third population, the program moved from being a summer enrichment, university-based context to being based throughout the academic year at Augustana High School.

When the program moved to Augustana, Project EXCEL became part of the standard college preparatory curriculum. We held planning meetings with the administration and faculty of Augustana, provided college-level materials in English, French, and German that mirrored those given to first- and second-year students at the local university, and provided in-service training on the EXCEL model to the college preparatory teachers in sophomore, junior, and senior level classes. We conducted interviews with EXCEL students, their parents, and these teachers as well as arranged classroom observations (English/German/French). While the research questions for the project as a whole remained unchanged, additional questions were formulated related to the experiences of EXCEL students in the English, French, and German classes within the regular school context.

Each of this book's remaining chapters focuses on these questions and provides a framework for describing the interactions between EXCEL and non-EXCEL students and teachers in these classrooms. In examining these questions, our focus became issues related to marginality and schooling. In the literature, these examinations have concentrated on how young people themselves define or are defined as being on the margins of school life (Apple, 1990; Cross, 1991; Hall, 1992; Hudak, 1993; McCarthy, 1990). Because the marginality of adolescents of color appears to be more, though not exclusively, bound up in issues of racism, several of the discussions center on how these adolescents construct their identities racially. Since our last cohort of students was exclusively African American and their school, Augustana, also overwhelmingly Black, we also wanted to see how, or if, race became a factor in the construction of an academic identity and, if so, what role it played. The in-class observations concentrated on teacher/student interactions; findings from those observations were informed by the work of Hudak (1993) and Foucault (1988). In his study of the process of self-representation, Hudak (1993) construes that some adolescents develop special coping strategies or inner monologues that enable them to "negotiate power relations within and through the margins. Neither monolithic nor static, the margins become for adolescents both site and 'technology' in the formation of racial identity" (p. 172). However, the racial frames of reference that inform their actions depend not only on how they define their situation but also on how they assess their interactions with others in complex social and cultural contexts. These interactions, in turn, when enacted within the cultural frames of reference related to school life, reflect the mythical norm that influences their border construction of social reality and the identity construction that occurs within it. Thus, the students' marginality or deviation from the mythical norm is part of a broader construction of social reality that takes into account "shared and contested perceptions, beliefs, interpretations, values, norms, and affects" (Figueroa, 1984 as cited in Hudak, 1993).

Foucault (1988, as cited in Hudak, p. 173) suggests that these strategies are not solely individualistic and idiosyncratic but rather represent the result of experiences within the cultural terrain mapped out by school life. For us, the need to investigate identity construction related to achievement motivation in a public school was also underscored by the persistent gaps between White and African American achievement, despite the proliferation of university/community-based enrichment programs. We also wanted our study to reflect the perspectives of the participants (EXCEL students, parents or guardians, and teachers). In analyzing our data, we asked the participants to read, critique and, finally, authenticate our interpretations. Employing this strategy as well as multiple data sources (i.e., school records, historical and archival information, yearbooks, newspapers, and student written work) provided a method of triangulation and the means to evaluate the credibility of our findings. In the following chapters, we discuss some of our findings. Beginning with Chapter 1, we examine through case studies marginality and representations of self through the experiences of two EXCEL students, one from Augustana and the other from Ryan. Chapter 2 treats how scholar identity emerged for EXCEL students within a tenth grade English class at Augustana High School. Chapter 3 centers on the relationship between teacher/student dialogue and achievement. Specifically, the chapter discusses how EXCEL students and their English and German teachers negotiated and constructed the meaning of scholar in their in-class interactions. Chapter 4 uses Jonathan Kozol's notion of "savage inequalities" as the framework for discussing messages of savagery and achievement in the EXCEL twelfth grade English and German classes. Chapter 5 provides an overview of what we have learned from our study. The implications of these data and the Project EXCEL study for further research into academic achievement for educationally disadvantaged African American adolescents are also discussed.

CHAPTER ONE
Framing the Experience of "Otherness": Marginality and Representations of "Self" Within Cultural Territories

Project EXCEL involved students who technically should not have been at risk but who were. By this, we mean that they had average or better than average grades (3.5–3.0, C+–B), had passed the standard basic skills test in their respective schools, were reading on grade level, and had a desire to attend college. While their socio-economic backgrounds differed, their school records would not have led a naive individual to label them at risk. What makes African American adolescents, who on the surface don't appear at risk, to be at risk? We believe the results of our longitudinal work are important in researching this question. This chapter presents findings from two case studies of academic ethos constructed during the fifth year of Project EXCEL. For the first six years, the project operated during the summer months of June and July at the University with high school teachers using course objectives and texts found in first- and second-year college courses in English, German, and French. In 1996, the program moved into a local high school, Augustana, as part of the regular college preparatory curriculum with a cohort of thirteen African American sophomore students. Since students from Augustana had participated in the previous summer projects at the University, the school administration, guidance counselors, and teachers were familiar with EXCEL. Students who met the admission criteria received a brochure describing the program and an application form from the guidance counselors. As in the past, the program operated for three years (sophomore through senior years), including a one-year follow-up of all students whether they attended college or not. The project goals centered on the development of academic ethos (scholar identity) in which the meaning of "scholar" for each participant was constructed from the perspectives and attitudes derived from academic study. To facilitate this process, the project's academic program concentrated on building the students' self-confidence and images of themselves as scholars, not as templates but instead as individually derived academic selves.

Using bell hooks' (1994) conceptualization of the dimensions of marginality and Hudak's (1993) theoretical framework which describes adolescent technologies of marginality, we sought to examine how two Project EXCEL students, Jeannine and Camille, used the margins as both the place and means of constructing their academic identities. Observations of and interviews with the two students, as well as interviews with their parents and teachers, were examined to analyze what strategies they developed and how they incorporated them (both in their regular classes and in the EXCEL project) in defining themselves as scholars.

The analyses of project data, including interviews with EXCEL participants, their parents and teachers (in the regular classrooms and in EXCEL) suggest that some EXCEL students do develop academic ethos (scholar identity) while others do not. Based on this finding, the research questions for this portion of our longitudinal study became:

1. How did individual students construct representations of self in relation to academic ethos?
2. What factors within the school and cultural settings influenced their construction of identity in general? and
3. What strategies did each employ to negotiate academic progress within and outside of the terrain of marginality (Hudak, 1993)?

We chose a qualitative case study method because of its compatibility with pattern theories (Lincoln & Guba, 1985, as cited in Merriam, 1988). Pattern theories offer explanations of a phenomenon only after a phenomenon is understood (Kaplan, 1964) and are analogous to Glazer and Strauss's concept of grounded theory in which similar data are grouped together and given conceptual labels. The case study approach also allowed us to examine our data in relation to a situation/context real model that takes a multidimensional approach to understanding achievement behavior (Katz, 1969 and Maehr, 1974, as cited in Castenell, 1984).

The case studies were constructed based on the following components:

1. Observations of students in English and foreign language EXCEL classes as well as in corresponding regular school classes;
2. Interviews with current and Pilot Project EXCEL students;
4. Interviews with parents of current EXCEL students;
5. Interviews with EXCEL teachers and regular classroom teachers; Analysis of standardized test scores (English/foreign language), writing samples (EXCEL and regular school classrooms), school records, and grade-point averages.

Equivalent data on a comparable group of non-EXCEL students were also collected to test the validity of emerging categories and themes. To arrive at emerging definitions of academic ethos and their relationship to academic achievement, we conducted inductive and independent analysis of the qualitative data using approaches suggested by Yin, 1989; Merriam, 1988; and Goetz & LeComptre, 1984. The data were then analyzed deductively to test the patterns and establish the categories in this chapter. Only those categories on which we achieved consensus are reported. The case studies offered in this chapter suggest that some students in EXCEL reconstruct their identities based on their individually developing understandings of being a scholar. These understandings are partially based on their experiences in the pre-college enrichment program (EXCEL) but also can be traced to experiences in their regular school classes, although the specific impact of EXCEL and their high school classes did not emerge from the data. The students' reconstruction involved some of the "inner monologues" to which Hudak (1993) referred in that the girls whom we describe, Jeannine and Camille, occupied positions of marginality in relation to components of the "mythical norm" (Lorde, 1984). We begin with Camille's story.

Camille

Seventeen-year-old Camille Lewis, who was reticent almost to the point of being withdrawn, completed her senior year at Augustana High School in

1992. When Camille entered Project EXCEL at the end of her freshman year, she had a grade point average of 2.5 on a 4.0 scale and had scored high on the Tennessee Proficiency Test with 92% in mathematics and 87% in language arts. This basic skills test was required of all eighth graders and had to be passed before a student could graduate from high school. The guidance counselors at Augustana recommended her for Project EXCEL because they identified her as an individual who definitely had college potential if she could be "motivated to get rid of her attitude." She completed her freshman year with an average of 2.5 and the following results in her college preparatory courses: English (B/C), Algebra (B/B), Physical Science (B/B), French (B/C), World History (C), and World Geography (C). Camille was described by one teacher as "physically beautiful, with short brown hair, a slender face and build, and light brown complexion." In fact, these characteristics were principal factors in her being selected as a cheerleader during her junior year. The same teacher also pointed out that she was academically capable but that her performance in class did not always reflect her potential. Similar comments were made in interviews with other teachers at Augustana, who remarked on Camille's "diffident attitude" and lack of participation in class discussions despite her frequent references to "going to college" and plans to "become a veterinarian." Once Camille entered our program, the EXCEL instructors expressed similar concerns. One of them, while noting Camille's special talent and interest in vocabulary study, found her to be resistant about participating in class and completing homework assignments.

During the sophomore and junior years, Camille continued to take college preparatory courses, and her grades exhibited dramatic fluctuations. The transcript of her courses and resulting grades appeared as follows: Mathematics, including Geometry (C/C), Algebra II (B), and Advanced Mathematics (C/C); English (B/B, D/C); French II (C/C), French III (D); Biology (B/C); Chemistry (D/C); U.S. History (D/C). While her grade point average during that period began as just slightly above average (C+), it dropped significantly in the first semester of the junior year to a 1.25 but improved to a 2.67 by the end of the next academic term, when she raised her college preparatory course grades from D to C and earned an A in Music and Driver Education. Despite Camille's stated interest in going to college, her performance belied the actual native talent detected by her teachers and suggested by her performance on the Tennessee Proficiency Test. During her initial interview for Project EXCEL, the project directors found Camille to be interested in participating in the program but rather constrained in her responses to questions about her activities in school and her plans for the future. These impressions were also supported by Camille's responses on her program application. For example, the question, "Why is a college education important to you?" elicited the following answer:

> I feel that if I want to be something in life and succeed that I need a good college education. I also feel that a college education is important if I want to go far in life and fulfill all my goals in life.

To the follow-up question on her reason for wanting to enter the program, Camille wrote:

> I am seeking acceptance into Project EXCEL because I believe this program will expose me to new resource materials used in college courses which will make college work easier for me. I will be able to fulfill my goals and succeed in life.

Her record of performance on national tests such as the PSAT (Preliminary Scholastic Assessment Test) and the ACT (American College Testing) revealed more inconsistencies that indicated that she was not working up to her potential. In the fall of her sophomore year she took the PSAT and the PACT (Preliminary American College Test). Camille's score on the PSAT was very low with the verbal score (23) ranking at the second percentile and the mathematics score (38) at the twenty-sixth percentile. She fared somewhat better on the PACT, obtaining a composite 15 (out of a possible 36) based on the following individual area test scores: English, 16; Mathematics, 19; Reading, 11; Science Reasoning, 15. During the fall of 1990 Camille participated with all EXCEL students in ACT/SAT training. She subsequently took the PSAT (Fall 1990) and twice took the ACT (June and October 1991). Her PSAT scores were low again, showing a slight improvement in the verbal (27, ninth percentile) and a drop on the math (34, eighteenth percentile). This was during the semester when her grade point average was at its lowest. She scored better, however, on the two sets of ACT scores, where her composite increased one point to 16 and then went up to 18. The following individual scores show that there was gradual improvement in all areas except Math, which she indicated was her favorite subject: English, 17, 19; Mathematics 16 (previously she had a 19), 19; Reading, 16 (up from 11), 17; Science Reasoning, 16, 18.

In 1998 Blacks who attended public high schools had a mean SAT composite score of 853, while the mean score of Whites was 1051 (*The Journal of Blacks in Higher Education*, Summer 1999). The composite ACT mean scores of Blacks in public high schools was 17.1, while the mean score of Whites was 17.1. While these scores are consistent with the national average for African American students, they were nonetheless inconsistent with both Camille's academic performance and the academic potential suggested by follow-up interviews with her teachers and counselors at Augustana. Her academic performance in school was fluctuating, but her scores on the national exams were improving. These fluctuations suggested that Camille possessed the abilities to perform at an even higher level but that she had not yet displayed or tested those abilities.

Camille's Performance in EXCEL

Just as her academic performance in school was incongruent with her abilities based on test assessments and teacher evaluations, so did her performance in EXCEL contrast markedly with her stated reasons for wanting to be in the program. At the start of the program, interview and observational data suggested that she was interested, energetic, and motivated to participate. For example, in interviews conducted at the end of the intensive summer sessions in 1989 and 1990, when asked what changes she would make in the program, she stated that she would make no changes and would "keep everything the way it is" (1989); she also maintained that "it [Project EXCEL] is helping me a lot in my writing skills" (1990) and that the French class was improving her proficiency in reading and speaking. On the other hand, her Project EXCEL instructors expressed increasing dissatisfaction with her work, which was often not completed on time, and with her weak commitment to the program, which was manifested in absences and unwillingness to participate in class discussions. Her two teachers in English and French talked about her being "very capable" but lamented that she showed little improvement and remained disinterested and unconcerned. When Camille failed to bring her grades up to the level required to remain in EXCEL (3.0) and showed little desire to cooperate with project instructors and directors on a plan to improve her grades or to demonstrate commitment to the program, she was counseled out of the project, as prescribed by the project rules. During the exit interview, her seemingly detached air and lack of interest in the process, and her curt, dispassionate responses appeared to confirm what had become apparent in her actions at school and in EXCEL: that she was not academically motivated and, more importantly, that she did not accept any of the responsibility for her academic failures. At the end of the interview, the project directors made recommendations to Camille about how to improve her academic and interpersonal skills, so that she might begin to achieve at a level consistent with her own assessment of her potential, but she responded to the recommendations with silence and gave no indication of her feelings.

Why does a student with an expressed desire to succeed academically and the recognized potential to do so fail to achieve? While the literature contains several responses to this question, our data on Camille yielded an intriguing finding. In interviews with Camille and her mother prior to entering EXCEL and during the program each indicated that Camille possessed the talent to become a veterinarian. A continuous theme emerging in both mother and daughter interviews was the conviction that given the right set of circumstances, this talent for veterinary medicine would be recognized and result in a college scholarship. For us, this conviction held by Camille and other students and their parents that potential alone is a more viable determinant of successful college admission and matriculation than demonstrated academic performance represented a strategy similar to those described by Hudak (1993) as "technologies of marginality." This belief denoted a way for these EXCEL students to construct an academic identity within an "existing context of power relations" (p. 173). In designing his study, Hudak adopted the work of Foucault (1988) in which the constitution of identity is not a matter of choice but rather a process imposed by the culture, society, and social group within which the individual is situated. In describing his subjects' "inner monologues," Hudak notes that these monologues were not invented by the subject but instead constituted ethical strategies through which they conducted themselves within already existing and socially established parameters—parameters which marginalized them.

"To deviate or to lie outside accepted norms has real social consequences for individuals who are labeled 'outsiders' and often find themselves ostracized [and] excluded" (Hudak, 1993, p. 173). For these individuals, then, constructing an identity within the margins that permits them to survive in contexts where they are powerless is an act of "radical social action" (hooks, 1990 as cited in Hudak, 1993, p. 174).

For some EXCEL students, we believe that what we have labeled "The Lana Turner Syndrome" (Welch & Hodges 1997) may represent one of Hudak's technologies, characterized as it is by the conviction that the recognition of potential and statements of intent are sufficient to assure realization of one's career or academic goals, provided the right set of circumstances exists to insure the individual's talents are "discovered." (A more detailed description of "The Lana Turner Syndrome" can be found in *Standing Outside on the Inside: Black Adolescents and the Construction of Academic Identity*, Welch & Hodges 1997).

As an example of an inner monologue that students hold with themselves, this belief or syndrome might be viewed as a strategy which students use to care for themselves in school, a context which requires the active construction of self by oneself within a negotiating field of power relations (Foucault as cited in Hudak, 1993, p. 173). We termed this belief "The Lana Turner Syndrome" because, for us, it mirrored an analogous view shared by several young aspiring actors and actresses during the 1930s. These individuals also confidently assumed that their talent would result in their being discovered by studio talent scouts. Attracted by the later disproved legend about the experience of actress Lana Turner, who was reputedly discovered sipping a soda at Schwab's Drug Store, they assumed that chance and potential would result in a greater opportunity for an acting career than drama training or the experiences afforded through bit parts. Those credited with having "found" Lana Turner reinforced this belief, by maintaining that they selected her because of her star potential even before they ever saw that potential realized on film. Similarly, Black youth are inundated with success stories like those of Aretha Franklin, discovered while singing in her father's church, or Hammer, whose rapping ability was first noticed on a street corner. Added to these examples are those superstars in athletics such as Michael Jordan and Magic Johnson, who achieved fame and fortune presumably because they were in the right place with the right stuff at an opportune moment. Because the media rarely discusses the hours of practice and discipline required of these talented athletes, movie stars, and recording artists, we believe that Black youth are left with the assumption that potential and circumstances account for their recognition. For Camille, convinced of her potential academic ability, the belief that she too would be recognized and rewarded suggested for us a reflection of "The Lana Turner Syndrome." The case study of Jeannine and her development of academic ethos provides an interesting contrast to the experience of Camille.

Jeannine

Fifteen-year-old Jeannine Kyle was a rising sophomore at Ryan High School when she applied for Project EXCEL. She had been selected by her guidance counselor for consideration because she met the minimum criteria and had expressed a strong interest in participating in the program. A White female diagnosed since the age of five with juvenile rheumatoid arthritis, described herself on the application as follows: "I describe myself as short, smart, kind, and nice and considerate of other people's feelings. I guess that is it." Although she began at Ryan High School, she completed her senior year at Hillside High School, one of two schools to which Ryan students were sent after the school closed as part of the desegregation agreement between the federally mandated Office of Civil Rights and the city. When Jeannine entered Project EXCEL at the end of her freshman year, she had a grade point average of 3.9 on a 4.0 scale and had scored at grade level on the Tennessee Proficiency Test with a 93% in Mathematics and 76% in Language Arts. In a pre-admission interview, when asked why and how she saw a college education contributing to reaching her future goals, she answered,

> I think a college education would help me because you need a college education to help you make something of yourself. And, I need one because I can't use my body. Because I can't get into any physical work because of my arthritis, so I need to get a college education where I can use my mind and I can have a good job.

Her 3.9 grade point average discussed earlier reflected the following results in her courses: English (A/A), Applied Math I (A/A), General Science (A/A), World History (A), and Reading (A). The English, Math, and

Science were classified at the Basic Level and were taken to strengthen her skills prior to entering the college preparatory level as a sophomore.

When asked during the interview process for EXCEL to talk about her future goals, Jeannine explained, "I hope to go into college and do something in computer technology and business management. Because I like computers and I would like to learn how to run a business. I would like to run a business. That's all." During the sophomore and junior years at Ryan, Jeannine took college preparatory courses and her grades continued to be well above average. Her transcript of courses and the results appeared as follows: Algebra (B/B), English II (B/B), French I (A/A), Biology (A/A), American History (B), and World History II (B/B). During the Junior year, her grade point average dropped to a 3.0 with the following results: Geometry (B/C), English III (C/B), French II (B/B), Chemistry (B/B), Marketing I (A/A), and a Co-opt Marketing course (A/A). After her transfer to Hillside School during the senior year, Jeannine's overall average dropped further to a 2.75/4.0 with the following grade results in college preparatory courses: English III (B), Algebra II (C), and U.S. History (C).

Her record of performance on the ACT, the national achievement test, improved over the three-year period. At the end of the sophomore year (1989), the overall verbal score was 16 and the overall math score was 13. On the PACT, taken during the same year, she attained a composite score of 13/36 based on the following individual test scores: English (13), Math (12), Reading (11), Science Reasoning (16).

During the junior year (1990), she took the PSAT with overall verbal (31/nineteenth percentile) and math (31/eleventh percentile). When she took the ACT near the end of her junior year, her scores showed improvement. Her composite was 15 with the following individual area test scores: English (13), Math (15), Reading (15), and Science Reasoning (17). She continued to score higher, and on the ACT test in the spring of her senior year she improved in all categories. Her composite score was 19 with the following area test scores: English (18), Math (16), Reading (22), and Science Reasoning (18). During this three–year period, Jeannine continued in the EXCEL English and foreign language courses during the summer and participated in a community service project with an adult professional as mentor during the last year. Her test scores were consistent with her academic performance and the academic potential suggested by follow-up interviews with her teachers and counselors at Ryan. While her grade point average dropped slightly with the increased difficulty in college preparatory courses, her scores on the national achievement tests (SAT/ACT) gradually improved with the most dramatic improvement occurring in reading.

Jeannine's Performance in EXCEL

Just as her academic performance in school and on national achievement tests remained consistent and strong, so also did her performance in EXCEL demonstrate a similar pattern. At the start of the program, interview and observational data suggested that she was motivated to participate even though she was somewhat shy and lacking confidence. For example, each morning the students were bused from the two high schools to the EXCEL program at the university. During the first year, Jeannine relied heavily on one other White student from Ryan for physical assistance in reaching classes and spent much of her time with this student during class breaks and lunch. The second student, Pam, was very confident and assumed this responsibility readily. However, by the second year of the program Pam's performance and attitude suggested a disinterest in EXCEL and school, while Jeannine's growing self-confidence, expressed in interviews, observational data, and increasingly strong academic performance, were paralleled by her stated commitment to Project EXCEL. For example, once Jeannine entered EXCEL, the English instructor pointed out her weaknesses in English vocabulary and occasional inattention to details in reading. Noting that Jeannine's weaknesses were more a question of lack of confidence than ability, her teacher added, "As she gains more confidence in her performance, this should improve." Jeannine worked "hard to 'brainstorm' a list of ideas, to organize a paragraph or essay" and "produced a good number of ideas for her essays." The EXCEL German instructor also made a connection between her confidence and her performance. She commented on how much improvement in skills and confidence she observed. The teacher said, "Unlike most of her group, this is her first experience with foreign language study. Her performance as well as her confidence continue to improve. Her oral proficiency is strongest of the four skills. Jeannine is creative and willing to try, but performs better in group work rather than independently."

During the junior year in school, she became vice president of the Key Club, took part in the school choir, and participated in SECME, the pre-engineering program to encourage women and minorities to enter engineering. She also made the school honor roll. When she graduated from Hillside High, members of the faculty from the former Ryan High School selected Jeannine to receive a $700 scholarship for outstanding academic achievement (money set aside for three rising seniors when Ryan was closed). Jeannine finished Hillside High and enrolled in a community college in the area with a major in computer sciences. She completed two years then transferred into the four-year university that sponsored EXCEL. During her first year, she achieved a 3.7 grade point average.

Jeannine's behavior and academic performance in EXCEL in her high school English and foreign language classes and in college suggested that she developed a scholar identity (scholar ethos). In the summer of 1990, when Jeannine was asked to give a definition of the word scholar, she replied, "A scholar . . . someone who doesn't necessarily go to college, a four-year college, but they go to a two-year college. And basically, just someone who when they get out in the real world, has a good job, a real good job. And is very successful." She was then asked to what extent she saw herself as a scholar? Her answer was," I'd say not a great person or good or anything. But I think I'm doing OK. I think I'm improving a lot." She then said, "I think I'll be a good scholar." In the summer 1991 interview, to the same questions she said,

> "I really wasn't sure of myself, I doubted a lot. You know, is that right? You know. But I really didn't try to push myself, you know. I may push a little and I would get a little ahead maybe and then I would say well I am ahead and I am going to stop and let everybody catch up with me. Now I think when I push myself, I just keep pushing because the further ahead you get the better off you are."

In her exit interview in 1992 Jeannine was asked what effect Project EXCEL had on her life and her answer was, "It's helped me to realize what college is like. What's it's all about, and how important it is and that you go to college and college education, and how much fun it would be. How good it would make you feel about yourself." Asked if she had changed as a result from being in Project EXCEL, she replied, "Yes. I think I'm more outspoken. I have more confidence in what I say and I look somebody straight in the eye when I tell them." The interviewer asked her how she would define a scholar and she replied, "Someone who is able to achieve what they set out to do. One who's able to meet that goal and go beyond it." She was asked if she knew any scholars and she said, "Yes. My friend, Pam, and me. I think everybody, really, that was able to stay in the program the four years. If they're there, then I think they're a scholar." She was asked what it would take for her to be successful in life and she replied,

> "I think for me to be successful in life I will complete my four years of college and I'll be on my own, taking care of myself, paying my own bills, doing my own thing and eventually working, if I wanted to go back into college or so forth, doing that."

Jeannine's academic performance in terms of grades and scores on national achievement tests supported the connection between this emerging identity and these quantitative measures of academic proficiency.

Few would argue that a sound academic foundation is crucial to the transition from high school to college, yet there is some question as to whether academics alone guarantee a student's graduation. While supplementary social and educational programs intended to redress the inequities considered major factors in the underachievement of minorities and those who are disabled, statistics report that African American disabled students continue to lag behind their White and/or able-bodied counterparts in completing college. While these programs do a great deal to ensure equal access to excellence and success, alone they do not and cannot counteract the impact of systemic sexism, classism, and ableism, nor can they dampen the forces of the current "market rationality" which, as Apple (1993) has observed, suggests that one is valued, that is, is a success, only if one produces, an outcome measured by the level of financial prosperity one attains.

Seminal studies of achievement motivation done by McClelland (1953), Atkinson (1966), and Maehr (1974) suggested that students achieve when they are motivated; moreover, these researchers contended that motivation must be intrinsic and supported by a strong sense of self-esteem. Based on these theoretical frameworks, policymakers concluded that providing access to adequate materials and skill-building techniques was the avenue to building that motivation. Neither the concept of intrinsic motivation, nor the problem of systemic oppression, accounts for the levels of achievement either in minorities or in those who are disabled. These phenomena alone cannot explain why some disadvantaged students achieve while others, given special attention and enrichment, nevertheless fail to progress. Lack of intrinsic motivation and the effects of oppressive conditions within the social environment, viewed either singly or together, do not adequately account for how processes within the schools, in concert with social issues and the individual student's personal development, combine to impact on achievement. For us, these unexplained issues call for a closer examination of the formation of an academic identity in the adolescents participating in our pre-college enrichment program, Project EXCEL, specifically, how these individuals evolved their definitions of the term "scholar" throughout their involvement in the project, and the relationship, if any, between that academic identity and academic achievement. In Jeannine's case the experiences of being female and disabled, in school and in EXCEL, were particularly important for us to examine.

An example of how Jeannine's identity continued to emerge after Project EXCEL occurred during a telephone conversation with one of the Project directors in spring of 1994, just before she transferred from the community college to the university. She talked about the community college's failure to accommodate her arthritis as required by the federal ADA. Specifically, school administrators would not change the location of a class that was physically inaccessible to her, instead requiring her to walk to the class. Jeannine told the project director that she had protested this action to Disability Student Services and because they refused to assist her in gaining a resolution, she transferred early. It should be noted that Jeannine did not transfer until she had exhausted every avenue to make the class accessible. Only after she determined that her actions had earned her the label "troublemaker," with the potential of this label affecting her academic standing, did she transfer. This is in striking contrast not only to Jeannine's personality when she first entered the program but also to Camille, identified early as academically talented both by teachers and test scores but whose performance later fell far short of expectations. Camille graduated from Augustana but attempts by the project directors to learn about what happened to her after graduation have been unsuccessful. Camille discontinued contact with the project directors, while Jeannine went on to complete a Bachelor's degree in Business Administration and a Master's degree in Education.

Conclusions

Emphasis on scholastic preparation without equal attention to a strong sense of academic identity ignores a significant factor in students' adjustment to college life (Allen, 1986, Fordham & Ogbu, 1986, Murray & Hernstein, 1994, Wexler, 1992, Vaz, 1987). Community/university/school partnerships must be developed to establish effective schooling based on a broader, global context, that is, one which addresses the complex social contexts that affect levels of achievement. The data from the case studies point to the need to continue research on the dynamics of social and cultural relations as well as representations of self that exist in school settings. Further, they argue for investigations of the impact of such dynamics on the construction of a scholar identity as a central component of academic achievement. In the next chapter we move from case studies to examination of the phenomenon of scholar identity within a whole EXCEL cohort based on their experiences in a tenth grade English class.

Note: Portions of this chapter appear in the book, *Standing Outside on the Inside: Black Adolescents and the Construction of Academic Identity*, Welch, O.M. & Hodges, C.R. 1997. Permission to reprint granted by SUNY, Inc.

CHAPTER TWO
Project EXCEL: Developing Scholar Identity Within a Community of Respect

Contemporary research on academic achievement and achievement motivation of educationally disadvantaged youth has generated questions concerned with the interrelationship of race, class, and gender, that is, how these factors are conceptualized by teachers and students and how students experience them with regard to their academic development. While much attention has been directed to the fact that these variables intersect at different points and in different ways for each individual (Andersen & Collins, 1992; McCarthy & Crichlow, 1993) and to the notion that race—neither fixed nor measurable but a "dimension of human representation" (McCarthy & Crichlow, 1993; Omi & Winant, 1994, p. 155)–is a complex and global concept, issues linking race and education remain at the forefront of discussions on school reform. Because of the history and complexity of problems associated with race relations in educational settings, several of those discussions focus on how students construct their identities with regard to race.

To the extent that they must deal with inequality of educational opportunity, that is, with limited access to the academic resources of their more privileged counterparts, disadvantaged students, in general, and African American disadvantaged students in particular, are even more acutely affected by variables that marginalize them. Thus, they are placed at the periphery of an educational institution that, based on an "alleged meritocratic system" (Mickelson & Smith, 1992, p. 360), presumably aims to support academic achievement. Disadvantaged students remain burdened by a number of factors, including schools inadequately equipped with materials and curricula that would better provide them with experiences routinely offered the best prepared students. Their undeveloped potential continues to be neglected because of grade point averages that do not rank in the top 10 percent or scores on standardized tests that do not exceed the norms. Moreover, they are sometimes, but not always, restricted by a lower income level that prohibits them from taking advantage of supplementary programs and materials to improve their skills. Thus, disadvantaged students are forced to adapt to an environment in which they are constantly entreated to achieve but in which they experience infrequent success and commonplace assaults on their competence. If they are to succeed, such students are faced with constructing an academic identity that not only fosters but sustains achievement despite factors that compromise and, in many respects, impede their progress. Increasing concern with the alarming lack of policies that deal effectively with the dynamics of social and cultural relations and strategies that address these difficulties (McCarthy, 1990) underscores the significance of identity construction as a factor related to academic achievement.

Project EXCEL

Project EXCEL examined the development of scholar identity (academic ethos) in college-bound sophomores as they participated in a university sponsored enrichment program of reading, writing, and foreign language study. The participants were students who self-selected for application to the program and who possessed the potential for completing college level work but did not have very strong academic profiles.

Tacit Theory

As was stated in *Standing Outside on The Inside: Black Adolescents and the Construction of Academic Identity* (1997), we acknowledge the influence of our own tacit theory on the study. Goetz and LeComptre (1984) have suggested that researchers' questions represent formulations that are grounded either explicitly or implicitly in their own personal experiences and perspectives. These experiences and perspectives, in turn, influence what these same researchers decide to investigate and the ways they think about those investigations. Similarly, our assumptions and biases influenced our decision to investigate academic identity formation in African American adolescents.

With current theories of identity formation in Black adolescents and our own experiences as the basis, we wondered whether the development of an academic identity might have had something to do with the construct called re-invention (hooks, 1994; Nieto 1994), a process which serves to both support and propel the individual toward higher levels of achievement. If so, might this re-invention be experienced by other adolescents? The study became the way to test our tacit theory that acquisition of the heuristic skills necessary for admission to college could not guarantee the successful college admission and matriculation of African American adolescents with potential. Even with the development of several well-intentioned enrichment initiatives to increase minority access to post-secondary education, increases in minority enrollment in colleges do not appear to keep pace with that of Whites. For example, the number of persons of color going to college paralleled increases in their numbers in the larger population. The college matriculation rate for White youths increased from 33 percent in 1981 to 40 percent in 1989 (U.S. Department of Education, 1997). Moreover, Oakes's (1985) work suggests that additional barriers to minority access exist. She notes:

> Most considerations of barriers to educational opportunity have focused on characteristics of students themselves as the source of the problem. Seen as products of disorganized and deteriorating homes and family structures, poor and minority children have been thought of as unmotivated, noncompetitive, and culturally disadvantaged. But there is another view . . . it seems the odds are not equal. It turns out that those children who seem to have the least of everything in the rest of their lives most often get less at school as well. . . (p. 4).

Oakes offers troubling rationales for the small minority enrollment in colleges and universities. This work and that of other researchers underscore the importance of understanding what internal and external factors may impact the ability of college-bound minority students to realize their potential and enter post-secondary institutions.

In this chapter we offer findings from one facet of the Project EXCEL study: the examination of the process of identity construction in EXCEL and non-EXCEL student participants in the tenth grade honors English course at Augustana High School. As we discussed in the preceding chapter, at the time of the study Augustana was a center city high school. Its population of 670 was 95 percent African American, with only one English class at each level designated honors/college preparatory.

Augustana resides in a business district of east Clarksville. The major road through this area boasts several churches, homes, a middle school from which Augustana derives the bulk of its population, business establishments, nightclubs, and a large subsidized housing development. Some of the nightclubs and the housing development periodically appear in the local newspaper as scenes of violence. At the time of the study, much of the main road was being repaved, making it bumpy and difficult to travel. A local community group was attempting to attract new business to the area, and a new convenience store had been built at the corner. Despite a small influx of new businesses, turnover remained high. Even so, there are some businesses considered community staples, including a dry cleaner and barbershop that have been in the same locations for twenty-five years.

Augustana, several blocks down this major road, is the product of an all White and all African American school mergers that occurred in the early 1970s. The school merger resulted in white flight, leaving Augustana with a predominantly Black population. Augustana stands out as a large brick building on the right side of the street, and trees line the grass in front of the sidewalk. The school is bordered on the right by a dry cleaner, with a funeral home and residences directly across the street. The school addition, containing a state-of-the-art basketball gymnasium, stretches Augustana to the corner. There is a large parking lot for faculty and staff at the right side of the building behind a wire fence. Three signs appear in the front yard of the school, two of which relate to past basketball championships won by the school, while the third is a marble sign that says a mind is a terrible thing to waste. Over the main door in the school building a blue sheriff's sign appears next to a yellow sign found in all Clarksville schools about the illegality of carrying firearms.

Conceptual Framework

The conceptual framework for this facet of EXCEL mirrored that of the entire study. However, since the project had moved from a summer enrichment program to become part of the college preparatory curriculum at Augustana, we wanted to know if, and if so, how scholar identity construction occurred within the regular classroom setting. In the English class we sought to understand how the EXCEL and non-EXCEL students as well as the tenth grade English teacher interpreted the meanings of and the expectations and motivations related to academic achievement in the class.

Such an investigation would allow us to test further the role, if any, of scholar identity in the academic achievement of these students. Thus, the following research questions framed this portion of the study:

1. How do the EXCEL students in the English class come to understand and respond to academic expectations?
2. How are the terrains of expectation (with respect to achievement and scholarship) negotiated?

Collecting and Analyzing Data

The way we chose to collect and analyze our data for this phase of the study represented our recognition of how "the other" has been constructed by those who conduct qualitative research and how we had on occasion "spoken of and for others while occluding ourselves and our own investments, burying the contradictions that percolate at the self-other hyphen" (Fine, 1994, p.70). Thus, in designing this portion of the EXCEL study, we were conscious that despite our shared racial identity with most of the students in Augustana and in the tenth grade English class, we needed self-consciously to "work the hyphen," that is, as Fine (1992) suggests, not to seek to "shelter ourselves in the text, as if we were transparent" (p. 74), but rather to recognize the hyphen between us and the EXCEL participants. This meant struggling with rather than acting as if there were no hyphen. To "work between" for us meant collaborating with EXCEL students, their parents, and teachers in the analysis and interpretation of our data and attempting through that process to resist "othering" even as we accepted that our "work would never 'arrive' but must always struggle 'between'" (Fine, 1994, p. 75). To facilitate the process, we chose participant observation as the primary methodology. In this role, the observer is present in the classroom but not participating or interacting with other people to any great extent during data collection (Hatch, 1985).

Because of the nature of the research questions, we decided to emphasize what occurred in the English classroom and the meanings derived from it for the students and teacher. Parent interviews, grades, writing samples, test scores, and school records, which are part of the larger study data, were not primary sources. Rather, greater emphasis was placed on observations of the students in English class and interviews with the EXCEL students and the classroom teacher. In this chapter, we focus exclusively on reporting the student and teacher comments during the class. Data also included articles from Clarksville's only local newspaper, two student newspapers, a school community newsletter, an Augustana student handbook, and the school's annuals.

Analysis of the data focused on the interaction patterns among all students (EXCEL and non-EXCEL) and the teacher, as well as the themes that appeared in discussions. Using key words, concepts, and patterns as brackets, categories emerged as well as related themes. This inductive method of analysis ensures that experiences are not labeled but rather are discovered, analyzed, and interpreted from data collected from the in-class observations and interviews. These data were analyzed deductively to test the themes discussed in the remainder of the chapter.

Tenth Grade Honors Class and Major Themes

The cohort of participants for this phase of EXCEL included thirteen EXCEL students and nine non-EXCEL students in the class. All students in the class were African Americans, except one female student and the teacher, who were European American. The Project EXCEL students were categorized within the class as honors and college preparatory, with one student labeled basic (he was later transferred out of the class). All others were honor students. The focus of data collection and the resulting data analysis were based upon how the students and teacher interacted during the English class, how knowledge was constructed in the class, and how the participants perceived themselves and their experiences related to discussions of text selections from *The Little Brown Reader* (Stubbs & Barnett, 1993), an anthology of essays used in first- and second-year university English classes.

The major themes that emerged centered on the classroom functioning as a community of respect. This community of respect, in turn, facilitated respect for self and others (Theme One), supported expression of opinions (Theme Two), and generated the establishment of identities (Theme Three). What happened in the classroom was driven by the community of respect and was influenced by what happened outside of the classroom in the school, local area, and the larger community.

Description of the Classroom

The English classroom was on the second floor of the school at the end of the hallway. The hallway was painted pale blue, the floors were clean, and the lights in the room bright. Brown metal lockers, with and without locks, lined the hallway. The class met in Room 213 from 8:45 to 9:50 A.M. In the class, the emphasis was on college preparatory reading and writing assignments and instruction was handled by one teacher, Ms. Young. In the class, the teacher evaluated and graded written work based on each student's academic level, but in class discussions, all students were encouraged to express their opinions, which were given the same weight. While these discussions were central to classroom activity and the interactions among students and teachers, in-class papers, role play, small group, and journal writing were also included.

Analyses of the Major Themes

The data suggested that a community of respect existed in the tenth grade Honors English class at Augustana High School. What occurred between the teacher and students was also influenced by what occurred outside of the classroom. The following discussion drawn from the analysis of the data focuses on how each of the three themes was enacted in the class.

Community Respect Facilitates Respect for Self and Others

Ms. Young was a white female of about forty years who had been transferred into Augustana as part of the Board of Education's plan to integrate faculty across the city. She had been teaching for over ten years and considered her placement at Augustana an opportunity to work with students whom she considered misrepresented as academically incapable. In interviews described later in the chapter, she discusses this misrepresentation. Attention to issues of respect for self and others was a priority. This attention was reflected in the patterns of interaction (both verbal and non-verbal) which occurred between the English teacher and the students. Initially, the respect was reflected in the greetings by name exchanged by the teacher and students at the beginning of each class. The significance of this ritual to the development of a community of respect was illustrated in a series of exchanges between Ms. Young and students before the class began.

Cynthia (one of the non-EXCEL honors students) arrives in class and observes, "Ms. Young, you not at the door." Luke (a Project EXCEL student) comes and asks about the last papers the students submitted. Ms. Young tells him they are in one of the trays next to the door. Regina (non-EXCEL student) arrives and warns, "Ms. Young, you need to control your door." Ms. Young responds, "I'm getting ready to come out there." Cynthia repeats her earlier comment, adding, "Good morning. Ms. Young, you're not at the door." Ms. Young responds, "I'm looking something up." Clearly, a ritual of greeting students by name and handling pre-class problems had been established in the classroom. Whenever that ritual was violated, either by the teacher's need to look something up or by other circumstances, the students in the class noticed and commented.

During class discussions, Ms. Young also demonstrated respect for students by asking questions, which invited a wide range of opinions, and also by sharing her own opinions with the students. This aspect of community was illustrated clearly in a discussion on faith related to one of the readings. The teacher and students had written in their journals and then began to talk about their experiences and opinions. Ms. Young shared two incidents in her life but reminded students, ". . . [this] is my own perspective, respect that, don't treat it as gospel, just that way for me." After her comments, Rachelle (EXCEL), Regina (EXCEL), Shanda (EXCEL), Keely (non-EXCEL), Diane (EXCEL), Victoria (non-EXCEL), and Richard (EXCEL) expressed their opinions about the role of faith in their lives. They also questioned other students in the class and each other. As the discussion developed, the teacher reminded the students about the expectation of respect for others:

"Let me interject, when we go over this section on religion . . . hostile feelers (at this point, the students laugh at the use of these terms), feelings [can] get hurt [if you're not sensitive]. When you make comments . . . everybody has to be respectful." At this point, Rachelle (EXCEL) says, "Oh, did I say it mean or something?" Rachelle mentions that talking about religion is like talking about race. Ms. Young says, "Ya'll have been real good about not being rude. When we're discussing religion, we need to be extra careful." One of the students, Linda (non-EXCEL) was a practicing Jehovah's Witness, and other students questioned her politely and expressed curiosity about the tenets of her faith. As they asked questions, Linda explained aspects of her belief calmly, responding politely to follow-up inquiries. Much later in the discussion, Ms. Young brought up the Crusades and jihad. Rufus (non-EXCEL) asked what the teacher's definition of jihad was, and Ms. Young replied, "Holy war." Rufus responded that it meant to struggle. Ms. Young answered, "I've been misinformed . . . thank you, Rufus."

This vignette was typical of the discussions observed in which the teacher and students shared a wide range of experiences without apparent strain and discomfort. In the choice of language, Ms. Young's expectation of respect for self and others was reflected as she thanked students for contributions to the discussion, apologized to them when she believed she had wronged them, and included "please" with any request, even reminders of appropriate behavior (e.g., "Ya'll listen, please."). Frequently, both Ms. Young and the students would say, "Excuse me," inferring that people were talking and not listening to what was being said.

Ms. Young was equally clear about the expectation that people would demonstrate respect rather than disrespect for others. Often she could be heard saying "We don't do that in this classroom" when students made comments that could be categorized as put-downs, or personal arguments, or laughing at or making fun of one another. On three occasions, Ms. Young asked students to leave the room when they got into personal arguments with each other. She also interjected the words "Be respectful" which seemed to imply a rule and expectation for both the students and herself. In turn, the students' behaviors suggested that they had internalized this rule, since they raised their hands to speak, took turns speaking, listened to the opinions of the teacher and classmates with whom they agreed or disagreed, and addressed each other by name when making comments. In the interviews, Ms. Young made these observations about demonstrating respect in class discussions:

> I want them to learn to respect each other, I mean me, of course, too, but to respect each other. Well, just as I would want to give them the respect for their opinions, I want other people in the class to do the same thing. Now whether you agree with their opinions or not, you need to let them say what's on their minds and we don't

put each other down, we don't tell each other to "shut up," and if someone says something that you disagree with, it's okay to disagree but don't put them down because you disagree. And, those are our general guidelines for discussions at the beginning of the year and after a while they get into it and they understand. I think that they like that. Well, you can't have a learning environment, if you don't have respect, I don't think . . .

These comments, in concert with the class observations, suggested that the expectation of respect for self and others was a core value that Ms. Young deliberately had set about to model and to require of the students. In turn, respect for self and others contributed to the community of respect by facilitating thinking and the expression of differing and occasionally controversial opinions (by both students and the teacher) during classroom interactions and in written communication.

Community Respect Supports Expression of Opinion

A second theme that emerged involved community respect facilitating the expression of a wide range of opinions on a variety of topics and subjects. Much of the class discussion grew out of the articles in *The Little Brown Reader*. One of these discussions centered on the prison system, and a spontaneous role play in which several students spent time in a cell while other students asked questions. After class, Rachelle approached the teacher and said, "Great discussion. We love this class." Ms. Young responded, "I thought you all said you didn't like it." Rachelle looked, gestured toward the work on the board and said, "We don't like all that."

Occasionally the students expressed their opinions about the book through moans and groans when Ms. Young asked them to take it out of their desks. However, soon most became quickly involved in the discussion, particularly since text selections were chosen to which the students related well. Students did not hesitate to convey their ideas to Ms. Young (e.g., Rufus's explanation of the word *Jihad*). Another example involved a discussion of the Studs Terkel essay, "Three Workers," in which the experiences of a prostitute were described. In the work, Regina found the word *intimacy,* which she said meant to her to have sex. Two other female students and Ms. Young emphasized that the word could also mean willingness to share innermost thoughts. As the discussion progressed,

Regina decided to get a dictionary, while Suzanne (EXCEL student) looked up the word in her thesaurus without prompting from the teacher.

Still another example involved the discussion of the Confederate flag. Rachelle and other students suggested that it symbolized slavery, while Ms. Young explained that while growing up the flag symbolized the South for her but that she had been enlightened. During this discussion, Ms. Young asked the students if they felt pride in being from Tennessee and they responded, "No." On this day, the students were quieter than on other occasions. Neither verbal nor non-verbal behaviors provided a rationale. Instead, toward the end of the discussion of the flag and other examples related to issues of free speech, Ms. Young said:

> All I want you [to understand] . . . (pause) . . . [It's a] hard time talking about difficult subjects. Basically what I want you to see . . . (pause) . . . [there are] so many gray areas. Everybody agrees this is okay, this is not . . . draw a line in what you think about it, not black and white related to freedom of speech.

Later she added, "This has been a difficult class period, but you all have been real patient." In a follow-up interview the teacher had this to say about the discussion:

> I found out a lot about them, you know, when I said, "Don't you feel pride being from the South and being from Tennessee?" and they were like, "Well, no." I was astounded, absolutely astounded. It was a very difficult discussion. The kids handled it pretty well. I thought, you know, they could have turned on me easily and I knew where I was going with that and that was a possibility, and I felt like they stuck with me that day at times when it was very difficult and I appreciate it but it was hard on all of us.

Another example of differing opinions expressed within the community occurred in a discussion of work, welfare, and child support. Some of the female students disagreed with the males about child support issues. As stated previously, students expressed opinions with varying degrees of frequency and intensity. At one point in the discussion, Alisha (non-EXCEL student), Shanda (EXCEL student) and a chorus of other female students became involved in a heated argument about mothers who work, go to school, and spend time with their children. Alisha told the other girls across from her to shut up and they retorted that she had an attitude. The girls' statement seemed aimed at reminding Alisha of the rule that differing opinions could be expressed without censure. At another point, Tommy (EXCEL student) was trying to add his opinion to the discussion and twice said, "Excuse me" when he was interrupted. Ms. Young reinforced Tommy's right to speak with "He has the floor."

In other discussions, when students appeared inattentive or off task, the teacher did not draw attention to the behavior verbally. Instead she utilized physical contact (placed her hand on a shoulder, made a pat on their back, or used her physical proximity to them) to ask a student to be quiet, to put something away, or to pay attention. Occasionally in the larger group or in the small student clusters, Ms. Young asked the students to be considerate, quiet, or to listen when their voices rose. From the beginning of the school year, she emphasized that the students must support their opinions with rational and effective thinking, written and oral arguments. About this emphasis, Ms. Young said:

> You know, I can't orchestrate a class discussion because I never know what other people are going to say and they may come up with more and different ways of looking at things that never occurred to me, and if I try to orchestrate it, then I'm taking away that spontaneity of their interpretation, and that's all part of thinking. See, if I do all the thinking, then they don't. So you have to let them take the ball and go with it.

An example of "taking the ball and going with it" occurred in a discussion on welfare. In a prior written assignment, students were asked to answer questions related to the readings, to write structured, five-paragraph essays and to write creative essays on the readings. Although grammar was not emphasized in the honors curriculum, Ms. Young reviewed grammatical problems that she found in the students' papers. In one instance, she asked the students to correct their papers before they would be given credit. On at least two other occasions, she talked about the importance of grammar on the writing test required in all eleventh grade Advanced Placement classes in the state. As Ms. Young assisted students in developing and refining writing skills, she emphasized respect for their opinions. As she handed back each paper, she mentioned to the students that most of her comments appeared on the front rather than in the body of the paper and that the papers did not take as long to grade as previous efforts (demonstrating that their mastery of grammar and punctuation was improving). Quietly, she added, "Please don't take it as I'm putting you down," and emphasized that she wanted to help them develop strengths in writing while working on weaknesses. She cited Shanda's feedback on two occasions that students needed more positive feedback on their work than they were receiving from the teacher. In the follow-up interview, Ms. Young reflected on her response to Shanda:

> Well, I wanted her to know that I listened to what she said to me and I didn't want to take up class time in the first instance because she was angry, and this could have degenerated into a "You don't like me" kind of thing, and I didn't want it to degenerate to that. I wanted to diffuse that and say, "Well, we need to talk about that later." I knew she probably was not going to come back, but if she did I would have talked about it to her privately and probably apologized that I didn't put a positive comment on her paper. Since she didn't, I felt like the next time I gave out papers that it would be a good thing for her to hear me say "I heard you and I'm sorry," and now she's away from the anger but it also empowers her . . . it empowers her when she feels that she has been slighted and can say "I've been slighted." And that is important in life.

In the class, respect for differing opinions appeared to support students' freedom and self-confidence to express their ideas and permitted them to practice appropriate ways to respond to those with whom they disagreed.

Community Respect Facilitates the Establishment of Identity

Community respect appeared to facilitate identity construction among the students. This finding emerged most strongly when students were asked to read aloud their papers about identity, followed by a student-led discussion about the issues that they confronted as they prepared the papers. In their identity papers, the students reflected on how they had changed, and several said they were more confident and had matured. The assignment required students to discuss in a creative essay how their identities had changed during the years. For the oral presentations, students stood at a podium, while the teacher sat at her desk and admonished the rest of the class to "demonstrate your utmost respect for your classmates."

Community Respect and Changes in Identity

Summarized below are phrases and quotes that reflected the students' perceptions of the changes in their identities:

> Cynthia (non-EXCEL): "I have more confidence...expressing myself more... and doing what is best for me."
> Linda (non-EXCEL): "I'm more interested in what is out there on other planets. My hopes and dreams are my identity."
> Regina (non-EXCEL): "I have learned to speak and think about others... and stopped being so hostile."
> Richard (EXCEL): Interested in going other places and finds humor in things, "has greater urge to compete," being comfortable arguing with caution.
> Roger (EXCEL): Doesn't sit in the corner like he did in the eighth grade. Plays sports and talks on the phone more, not too many people like his friends but he does "because they are my people." Says that he "takes nothing from no one."

As students read, Ms. Young provided feedback and their classmates applauded. At this point, the teacher said, "Ya'll are doing a good job. By the way, you've matured a great deal."

> Diane (EXCEL): "I am a Black woman who has achieved a lot, loves and gets along better with her mother."
> Julius (EXCEL): Moved here from Alabama and has a job. He has learned to go places he never thought about. Says he is being more competitive.
> Shanda (EXCEL): Says that people insist that she has options open to her, but that she is hardheaded. She talks about family support and wonders what will happen and thinks about where she is going to college. She is more outspoken now and says she doesn't mean to be rude, but she doesn't want to talk about certain things.
> Luke (EXCEL): Says that he is interested in mind states, not identities. Identities are superficial. He sees himself as older, wiser, a unique individual self.

Students applauded at the conclusion of the feedback on both presentations. Keely, Rufus, and Rachelle (non-EXCEL students) were not there to present papers. Several students mentioned having more confidence, being expressive, and being more mature. Ms. Young encouraged the class to continue to take stock of themselves and their goals. "[It's a] good way to give yourself a pat on the back."

Identities Related to Community of Respect

Two of the three discussions that occurred in the classroom suggested that student perceptions of identity were closely related to the community of respect. The first of these involved feelings of pride connected with being from the South or Tennessee. Students did not seem to have strong connections with the larger communities in which they live. This was illustrated in the major topics and transitions, which occurred in the student-led discussion.

The discussion focused on the school system and the different ways that Augustana and its students are represented in Clarksville. Keely says, "I understand that we're a Black school . . . put us on TV . . . [there is] more going on." Ms. Young suggested that being a Black school and having more television exposure were not necessarily connected and encouraged Keely not to think of herself or of the school negatively. Keely responded, "That's not how I was making…" (and was interrupted by other students' verbal affirmations). Ventura added, "People down our school, expect us to do bad stuff." She mentions specifically how the school is presented on television. LaTisha began to talk about area high schools and said, "We are the only predominantly Black high school left in the county…" Ms. Young interrupted, saying, "I don't want you to even think along those lines…" LaTisha nodded and later placed her head down on the desk, ending her involvement in the discussion.

In the continuing discussion, Ventura mentioned how "bad kids" were sent to Augustana, those who were frequently involved with the juvenile justice system. Shanda expressed similar sentiments. Ms. Young asked, "How can you change the school's image?" The students offered examples of positive activities occurring at the school, including the science fair, and Ms. Young mentioned that she had seen the names of students in the class and from the school in the local newspaper. Another student countered that the school was mainly recognized for its athletics (football and basketball teams). Luke said, "[I] was going to say that…" and added that athletics was mentioned more than anything. He continued by pointing out that when Ryan (a school which began as all White and later became interracial—60 percent White and 40 percent Black—and had been closed two years ago) was open, all that was discussed about either school was their rivalry in athletics, not academics. Ms. Young introduced the topic of academic identity, observing that in the first two years she taught at Augustana, no male senior qualified academically to become "Mr. Augustana," an award given for academic excellence. Glancing pointedly at a group of male students, she added, "I know we have kids who will qualify."

The discussion continued with issues of power, representation, and action becoming topics. Nicole said that voting for class officers to address Augustana's image problem was "favoritism to me." Luke replied, not loudly but clearly, "I did not vote." Ms. Young said, "I know you feel powerless at times," but questions whether the students would want teachers rather than themselves to select candidates or officers. The students expressed frustration with how little had been accomplished by the current class officers. The class began to brainstorm ways that they could increase class activities. Luke mentioned wanting to go on field trips as a possibility, and Victoria voiced her desire to make a senior trip. Ms. Young responded, "Don't sit back and wait and blame everybody else." Again, students blamed sponsors and officers who did not appear to be taking responsibility. To help the students think of the problem differently, Ms. Young asked, "Shanda, you play basketball. What would you do if someone on the team mishandled the ball?" Shanda replied, "Get it," and continued, "I'm going to tell it like this about taking the ball, can't take too much with a referee." Shanda then asked Ms. Young if she would be their sponsor but was told that Ms. Young was already the ninth grade sponsor. Nicole and Keely said that they wanted to form committees. Luke and Shanda noted that other people might take the credit for their initiative and for the work, but Ms. Young emphasized the importance of the end result. Luke talked about "getting started" and field trips. In an authoritative voice, Victoria turned to him and said, "Pay first, then get buses." During the discussion, the teacher had remained in front of the room. At this last comment, however, she laughed. As the discussion moved to other activities, Nicole asked if the students could have a meeting of "the whole tenth grade class" in Ms. Young's room, and Ms. Young replied, "Yes... I am happy to help you, I want you to do well and to have things for yourselves." Until the bell rang, the students formed committees.

In addition to demonstrating how the students moved from discussion to action, this vignette also reflects their frustration with the representations of the school, its students and what actions they would like to take to secure better opportunities for themselves. In the follow-up interview, Ms. Young expressed her views about Augustana's and the students' images:

> I think the population at large sees Augustana as a failure as far as schools are concerned. I think they see it with fear. I think they associate Augustana with violence and ignorance. I just want it to be perceived as another high school in the county. I mean it's that simple. I feel the kids sometimes see themselves the way Clarksville at large sees Augustana, not the [one section of the city] but Clarksville at large. And I have had many experiences where I have gone to people and they say where do you teach? And, I say Augustana, and they go, "Oh," you know like, "I feel so sorry for you." And it really bothers me. It bothers me; because we've got some very bright, bright kids here. I hate for them to be perceived that way, and I feel that a lot of the kids perceive themselves that way because of that kind of pressure. The more we're out in the community, the more we participate in academic contests instead of just sports contests, the more we make a name for ourselves and a good name [the better our image will be]. You know if I could do anything single-handedly, if I could do that, you know, we could go out in speech contests and things of that nature and make a name for ourselves and people [would] say, "Oh, my gosh, there's somebody from Augustana, you gotta be good."

Conclusion

Our data suggest that the community of respect found in Ms. Young's class facilitated the construction of student identities. Although aware of the pressure and prejudices that circumscribe the wider community's perceptions of them and Augustana, the students saw themselves as worthy of respect. The expression of differing opinions fostered during class discussions assisted them in learning to understand each other and in reflecting on the emergence of each evolving identity. An area for continued study involves the significance of the interface between the school community and the larger community within which it is situated and how that interface influences the students' continued identity construction. This ethnographic study is currently under way as a part of the project.

The participant observations in the tenth grade Honors English class at Augustana High School suggested the establishment of a community of respect that facilitated respect for self and others, supported the expression of individual opinions, and, through the process, resulted in the construction of identities. With both EXCEL and non-EXCEL students, Ms. Young had created and shared an environment that was shaped by respect. For the students, what occurred in the classroom was influenced by this community of respect and also by what occurred outside the classroom. A related and critical finding was that students, whether EXCEL or non-EXCEL, did not seem to identify with the larger community within which they lived and pursued their education. The data from this phase of Project EXCEL underscore the need to continue research on the dynamics of social and cultural relations, as well as the representations of self that exist in school settings. Further, they argue for investigation of the impact of such dynamics on the construction of a scholar identity as a central component of academic achievement.

In Chapter three we continue to look at how teacher/student dialogue contributes to EXCEL student and teacher definitions of achievement in the eleventh grade English and German classes.

CHAPTER THREE
Student-Teacher Dialogue and Achievement: Negotiating Meaning and Constructing Scholar Identity in English and German Classes

This chapter examines one political aspect of schooling for African American students, that is, the dual messages about achievement conveyed to them through their experiences as individuals and as a group in their eleventh grade EXCEL English and German classes at Augustana. Seven EXCEL students participated in the Advanced Placement English class. The remaining four were placed in the College Preparatory course. In the foreign language courses, six EXCEL students took German II/III and the remaining five took French II/III. The English teacher was an African American female, while the French teacher (female) and the German teacher (male) were European Americans. All of the students (EXCEL and non-EXCEL) in the English and foreign language classes were African American.

The preceding chapter described how EXCEL students developed definitions of achievement within their tenth grade English class. This chapter centers on the EXCEL students in the eleventh grade English Advanced Placement class and the German class. The English class was chosen because it represented the only eleventh grade Advanced Placement English course offered at Augustana High School. Students permitted to take the course had to meet the county's criteria for advanced placement courses and be recommended by their tenth grade teacher. The chapter also focuses on the EXCEL students in the German II/III classes. Because of uneven scheduling and the maternity leave of the French teacher, the French class met for only a half-year with the regular teacher. The substitute teacher, also European American, who was hired for the second semester used primarily written work and drills in class rather than oral communication exercises. For this reason, data collection for the French class was too inconsistent to identify themes. By contrast, the German class met for the full year, and so our analysis centers on the interactions in this class along with those in the Advanced Placement English class.

Research Questions

In this phase of the study, we sought to understand how the students in EXCEL and the English and German teachers interpreted achievement and scholarship in the classroom. We also wanted to see how these interpretations related to the messages (direct and indirect) given by teachers in their interactions with EXCEL students. Only through such interpretations could we further our study's investigation of academic ethos, our own understanding of the meaning of academic achievement for these students, and how those messages related or did not relate to their individual achievement in class. Therefore, the following questions represent extensions of those presented in the preceding chapters:

1. How do the EXCEL students in the English and foreign language class (German) come to understand and respond to academic expectations?
2. How are the terrains of expectation (with respect to achievement and scholarship) negotiated for both EXCEL students and their teachers?

Collecting and Analyzing Data

Because of the nature of the research questions, we used classroom observations and interviews with EXCEL students and their teachers as the primary data sources. We also collected equivalent data on non-EXCEL students to test the validity of emerging categories and themes. The focus of data collection and the resulting data analysis were based on how the students and teachers interacted in the English and German II/III classes and how the EXCEL students perceived themselves and their experiences as they related to topics covered in their Advanced Placement English class and to the study of a language and culture different from their own.

The data were analyzed deductively to verify the patterns and establish the categories reported in the findings. Using key words, concepts, and patterns as brackets, categories emerged and within them themes. This inductive method of analysis ensures that experiences are not labeled in advance but rather are discovered, analyzed, and interpreted from data collected from the in-class observations and interviews. These data were then analyzed deductively to test the themes discussed in the remainder of the chapter.

Findings

The findings presented in this chapter suggest that EXCEL students construct and reconstruct definitions of achievement based on their individually developing understandings of being a scholar. In the English and German classes, these constructions center on differing and sometimes conflicting messages (both direct and indirect) related to achievement and scholarship (Theme One). The duality of these messages, in turn, resulted in negotiated student behaviors and experiences in the classroom (Theme Two). Finally, the standpoints (Hill-Collins, 1990) of the two teachers were revealed and expressed through direct and indirect messages on achievement and scholarship conveyed to students (Theme Three). As in the tenth grade English class, for the students, what occurred in the classroom was also influenced by the perceptions and expectations conveyed from elsewhere in the school, the larger community, and the media.

Description of English and Foreign Language Classrooms

The English classroom was on the second floor of the school at the end of the hallway. It was large with two entrances and contained a stage, one computer, and a storage area. The teacher's desk at the front of the room had a podium in front of and to the right of it. There was also a stage area where students who were late to class were required to sit. One small bulletin board was used by Mrs. Wright, the English teacher, to display articles about the school and the students. Posters about writing could also be found throughout the room. On the remaining bulletin board at the back of the room, labeled "The Write Stuff," Mrs. Wright had placed student written work. By contrast, neither the French nor the German teacher had his/her own classroom. Instead, each had to move from one vacant classroom to another each period, transporting whatever was needed on a portable cart.

At the time of the observations, the local school system had just instituted block scheduling in the high schools, and the semester-length, 90-minute English class (configured to be the equivalent of one year of 50-minute classes) and the full year, 90-minute, French/German classes (configured to be the equivalent of two years of 50-minute classes) represented the change.

Instruction in the English and German Classes

In the English course, Mrs. Wright wrote assignments frequently on the board, daily recording on it the date and "word for the day" with a corresponding definition. The VCR and monitor were used for presentations that illustrated or introduced study topics, while an overhead projector in concert with the board were employed for exercises and discussions. An audiotape allowed students to listen to full and abridged versions of Shakespearean plays. Several textbooks and novels, *The Crucible, Animal Farm, Jubilee, The Great Gatsby,* and *Black Boy,* were used throughout the semester. These were supplemented with a guide for writing research papers and a magazine emphasizing writing.

The students and teacher went to the library frequently and were given an award for being the best class of the semester in library use. A few students (both EXCEL and non-EXCEL) participated in tutoring with the Title I reading teacher to improve their on-demand writing. Project EXCEL students Jeff, Roger, Luke, and Ventura worked as tutors. Rules were not displayed in Mrs. Wright's room, although she frequently referred to understood behavior and work expectations.

German Class

The German II and III classes were designed to develop language proficiency in four skills, i.e., reading, writing, listening comprehension, and speaking, as well as to foster cross-cultural awareness through study of the target culture. The teacher, Mr. Franklin, evaluated and graded homework, quizzes, tests, and class participation to determine the grade for the class. All Project EXCEL students (one student in the class was not in Project EXCEL) were required to take part in one extracurricular German activity, the German Spring Festival (*Frühlingsfest*), an annual statewide competition of high school students studying German. To supplement written exercises on grammar and vocabulary, the teacher made use of games to reinforce learned material and to practice new concepts. Students were sometimes placed in a semicircle to enhance interaction and participation.

German was first included in the curriculum at Augustana with the introduction of Project EXCEL, which provided funds to pay for a German instructor, since the school system could not offer Augustana a position for a German teacher at that time. The class was open to other students not in the project but electing to take German. Because of the funding provided by the project, students had the opportunity to take German every semester under block scheduling, as opposed to one semester per year for students in French and Spanish. In the class, the teacher graded written work based on each student's academic level, but in class discussions all students were encouraged to express their opinions, which were given the same weight. These discussions were central to classroom activity and the interactions among students and teachers. Written class papers, role-play, small group, and journal writing were also included.

Conflicting Messages Related to Achievement and Scholarship: The Advanced Placement English Class

In the English class, three messages that were communicated strongly emphasized the importance of (a) producing college-level work in the Advanced Placement Class; (b) preparing oneself for college, even if it's not an option; (c) understanding the experiences of people who have paved the way for the students and/or impacted their lives. Excerpts from in-class observations illustrate these messages:

> "This is AP, when I give you instructions I expect you to follow those to the letter."
> "Prepare yourself for college as if (you) are going."
> In referring to the ACT, "Colleges want to know your ACT score and you want to do well on the ACT."

The teacher goes on to mention that environmental and cultural bias may enter in, but students can't use them as an excuse. She says:

"There's no Black math."

"Don't wait for anybody to teach you. Make use of the library."

"Where's your book? [Not having your book] is like going on a picnic with no food."

"How well you speak is going to make a big difference in your life."

"I want you to listen to this . . . you are fortunate to be educated and know what people are talking about."

Mrs. Wright underscored these messages by being in place herself at the very beginning of class when the students appeared and by varying her position in the class. To reinforce the importance of "flexing their thinking muscles," she included several kinds of writing exercises; required students to have their materials (books and assignments) or suffer point deductions; and used journals, memoir statements (which she posted daily), "fish bowl" conversations in which students watched each other, and the "present, stand, and deliver" activity in which each student took a position, offered supporting evidence, and was challenged by other students on the validity of the evidence. In assigned small groups, she required students to cooperate and collaborate on answers. Time was an important element. If students were not in their seats when the bell rang, they sat on the stage. A timer was frequently used for tests and other kinds of exercises. Further, students were told how much time remained for them to complete work. During several observations, Mrs. Wright mentioned that the students didn't have enough time to do the things she would have liked, especially when completing research papers. She expected students to explain as thoroughly as possible their positions and not apologize for the inadequacy of those explanations before they began.

In Mrs. Wright's class, several discussions focused on the school, the students, and comparisons with other schools in the area. A great deal of discussion occurred after an unfavorable comparison of Augustana with a more affluent school with a largely European American population. Students insisted on writing letters to the editor, even though none of the letters ever appeared in the newspaper. During the first semester of the school year, a shooting occurred outside of Augustana. The only local newspaper in Clarksville recorded accounts of the gang-style slaying of an African American suspected of dealing drugs. Although neither the slain drug dealer nor his alleged killers were students at Augustana, the incident made front-page news and was reported on all three of the local news stations with accompanying pictures of the school. To counteract this, Mrs. Wright invited former students to talk with the class. She also compared her experiences at the old all—Black Augusta High School and in the community. She reminded the students that they were not dealing with the blatant kind of discrimination that others had endured before them and that others had suffered for them to get where they were.

A particularly striking example of this strategy occurred when Mrs. Wright invited a middle-aged African American male teacher from the school to her class to discuss his participation in the Million Man March. Although students were receiving positive reinforcement in Mrs. Wright's class for pursuing academics, conflicting messages were presented by the media, where the focus was on the inadequacy of their school in comparison with its peers and the incidences of crime rather than scholarship. Students were also aware of these contradictions:

> "They put less money in black schools," one student remarked during the discussion of the newspaper article comparing Augustana with its peer school. "We have a new gym but other parts of the building are crumbling." "Shipley, Holt, Sharp and Thompson (other schools in the community with low black enrollments) get publicity that tends to be positive. [When they talk about Augustana], they mention shooting and fighting."
> "The families of Shipley, Holt, Sharp, and Thompson have more money and get more done in their schools than people in this school."

Duality of Messages Resulted in Negotiated Terrains of Expectations

The duality of messages regarding achievement was most strongly supported in student interviews conducted at the mid point of the school year. For the EXCEL students, English was most often mentioned as the class causing them difficulty. Despite their discomfort, six students said that they were pleased with the quality of the class, even though they all agreed it was very challenging:

> "In English, I feel pressured . . . I think it's going to help me a lot."
> "She helps us, she motivates us to do better . . ."
> "In the two years I've been here, I haven't had that much work demanded of me, and she's pushed for a lot of effort."

Students who were unhappy with the quality of the English class said:

> "She's just plain rough."
> "English is too hard."
> "English is frying my brain."

These statements were confirmed in the monthly early-morning meetings between the students and one of the EXCEL project directors. Frequently, students mentioned the demands made of them by the English teacher, including multiple revisions and drafts, heavy deductions for inadequately prepared or late work, and expectations that some stated they couldn't seem to meet.

> "Other teachers are more understanding. She's never pleased."
> "We have to complete novels quickly. I'm used to more time."
> "She don't accept excuses or apologies."

In one instance, prior to an observation, a student sent his father in with a late paper. Mrs. Wright apologized but told the father she would not accept the paper because his son had sufficient notice to complete the assignment on time.

Scholar Identity

Student identity represented another negotiated terrain for EXCEL participants. In the interviews three common perspectives emerged about scholars. Four of the five students felt most like a scholar when they maintained a healthy balance in their lives:

> "A mature way of looking at things like schoolwork-like you have to be on top of your schoolwork, pay attention in class, be respectful to teachers and classmates."
> "Act professional type attitude."

Also mentioned were leadership ability, attitude, and self-respect. For other students, the ability to do well academically was a major factor, while for others, just doing the best they were capable of and having a stick to it attitude were sufficient indicators.

Students were also asked to identify who came to mind when scholars were discussed. Among the names was one of the EXCEL students, an African American male who later would be named valedictorian, Mrs. Wright, Colin Powell, Michael Jordan, Richard Wright, mothers, and fathers. In each case, the students gave rationales for their choices, which closely paralleled their definitions of what it meant to be a scholar. These data suggest that for EXCEL students' definitions of scholar and scholarship continued to be negotiated and renegotiated within contexts both personal and academic.

Teacher Standpoint on Achievement and Scholarship

In both the English and German classes, teacher standpoint on achievement and scholarship was enacted for the students.

Mrs. Wright, the English teacher, is a forty-eight–year–old African American who grew up in East Clarksville. As a teenager, she had attended Augusta High School, the all–Black school that had been merged with its White counterpart to form Augustana High School. She graduated from Augusta at age sixteen. From there, she attended Clarksville College, a historically Black institution in the community, from which she graduated. After teaching middle school in Clarksville and another city in the state, she returned to the major university in Clarksville, where she received her master's degree. She had taught French, English, reading, history, and Spanish. She also chaired the English Department at Augustana and had taught for twenty-five years. In interviews, Mrs. Wright described herself as:

"just a teacher who is teaching students . . . I will try to teach them the best I can. I worked hard in the past and I intend to continue to do that. Uhm, there's so many factors in public education that tend to thwart a lot of things that you have a desire to do. I know that sometimes it's not that the students don't want to do . . . how they are placed as far as their self-esteem is important. Some of the students who don't have the basics, I'm sorry that we don't have the personnel where classes could be smaller, and those students, you could give them the additional help that they need."

In the classroom, Mrs. Wright demonstrated her standpoint that "education must become important" by placing words and definitions on the board that illustrated "striving toward excellence" (e.g., *resolve* –

determination, fitness of purpose). "The basis of all persuasion is an argument: An opinion supported by reasons, which are, in turn, supported by evidence. To write convincingly, you must be able to judge how effective your argument is." She followed this definition with a lesson in which she offered various statements with which people would agree (e.g., fathers should take care of their children) and required students to support or refute them. As positions were offered, Mrs. Wright provided critical feedback on content and grammar:

> "What is a valid argument and solid reasons?"
> "Don't just restate positions."
> "What is the verb form of conversation?" Student replies, "conversate." Teacher responds, "Converse." Student surprised adds, "In rap songs, they use "conversate."

Mrs. Wright also required students to give each other feedback, noting that the ability to take and give critical assessments was an important skill. Even in the last week of class, she emphasized her support for academic work by holding a Book Talk in which each student selected and discussed a book read during the semester that came from a reading list provided by the teacher. The following list of titles was generated:

> LaTisha: *The Jungle*
> Nicole: *The Scarlet Letter*
> Alisha: *The Awakening*
> Shanda: *Jane Eyre*
> Victoria: *A Death in the Family*
> John: *Hiroshima*
> Tommy: *Crime and Punishment*
> Regina: *The Bluest Eye*
> Jeff: *The Old Man and the Sea*
> Alan: *Cry, the Beloved Country*
> Ventura: *Animal Farm*
> Diana: *Wuthering Heights*
> Rachelle: *The Invisible Man*
> Rufus: *The Grapes of Wrath*
> Melanie: *Our Town*
> Keely: *Gulliver's Travels*
> Cynthia: *Pride and Prejudice*
> Richard: *A Portrait of the Artist as a Young Man*

Students described the content of each book and their own reactions to them. At the end of the hour, Mrs. Wright was smiling.

The German Class: Conflicting Messages Related to Achievement and Scholarship

In the German class the teacher placed emphasis on individual student needs. Because the class was small (eight in the fall; and seven in the spring), he was able to provide a great deal of attention to each student. Mr. Franklin stressed the importance of doing this in an atmosphere that starkly contrasted with the more reserved and more easily managed (from a behavioral perspective) college classes he previously taught. In an interview, he noted:

> I have to realize that it's not the college environment, and if I walk in and it's not total silence, that's not a failure. As long as I can get them to do their work, and stay involved, then I can accept that it's not like a college class.

Indeed, through the use of a variety of games and written exercises that focused on student interests, and activities requiring small group work, he did get them to attend to the task at hand and to stay involved. As stated previously, Mr. Franklin maintained a relaxed classroom atmosphere. Students talked to each other about class-related work as well as events or issues in their own individual lives. Yet, the student interview data suggest that the latter did not detract from their enthusiasm for the class. Indeed, the students particularly liked comparisons in class discussions related to cultural differences between Germany and the United States. For example, in a follow-up interview about Project EXCEL classes, Richard observed that he enjoyed the German class because "Mr. Franklin makes sure he's explained everything thoroughly to you and he makes it fun."

Although Mr. Franklin frequently had to force them to return to their task, he most often did so with seemingly minimal effort. Because of their apparent trust in him and his often-expressed confidence in their abilities, he appeared to be able to lure and then completely engage them in the assignment at hand. Thus, when they first started reading a sixteenth-century story that ended with a joke, they were very skeptical and declared that it was a *doof* (colloquial German for stupid, ridiculous). After they gradually became used to the dialogue and comprehended enough to speculate on the turn of events, the students became excited about acting it out as a skit. As the students worked together translating the story, discussion continued rapidly. Finally, one student proposed that the story be adapted to a skit for the German Festival competition:

> Student: "You entered us for a skit . . . If we did a play, you wouldn't have all these words. You'd just need the dialogue."
> Another student: "I'm not doin' it."
> Mr. Franklin: "Read on. You can do it. I have confidence in you."
> Another student: "I'm reading."

Several minutes later they were involved in a lively discussion about how to stage it as a skit. They discussed how they could make it into a little play, observing that they needed three characters and a horse.

> "We could make Brian be the horse," suggests a student, volunteering the one student from German II who did not continue with German III.
> Shanda speaks up, claiming, "I want to be the student."

Jeff and the others are all talking. Suzanne volunteers to be the wife and Richard has his hand up to volunteer.

Frequent quizzes were used to develop vocabulary and to test concepts of grammar. When they read together in class, the teacher further reinforced familiar vocabulary by using it to explain in the target language words which they had not yet learned. The students responded well to this, although it was not incorporated often enough to encourage them to answer and ask questions in German. Again, while the teacher consistently praised them for how much they had learned in German and for their talents as language students, he, in some cases, stopped short of forcing them to the next higher step, presumably because of the perceived difference between his college class (predominantly European American, middle-class adults) and the high school ones (African American, center city teenagers). Reflecting on how he felt differently about teaching at Augustana in comparison to teaching college students, Mr. Franklin observed:

The classroom environment—dealing with the students . . . I guess, college students are pretty quiet; one of my big goals with a college class is to get them motivated and get them going, which I'm good at because I'm pretty active and enthusiastic in class. With the high school class, it's often you have to calm them down and get them to concentrate and get their attention, which is different. And they—you have to deal with their moods a lot more than you do with college students. [College students] kind of keep that stuff outside the classroom. Here I have to deal with that every day. And they'll tell me exactly what they feel. If they are frustrated with an exercise, they'll tell me it's stupid, they'll just let me know. Or if they think an exercise is too easy, they'll tell me. They will speak their minds and tell me how they feel. And so every day I'm dealing with situations, encounters with students that I've never dealt with. And so every day, I'm kind of dealing with things on my toes.

The students were reminded—and seemed to recognize—that they had considerable talent, and the German teacher made it clear that he was very much committed to meeting their individual needs. In his interactions with them he was consistent about his high expectations and, as a result, the students seemed to be motivated to excel. They continued to do so in the face of experiences in other classes, which offered negative messages and conflicting discourses. In one example, two female students commented on the attitude of a teacher in another class who was aware that they were studying German.

Suzanne: "You know, he only knows one word in German, *schwarz* [black]. He asks me every time what *schwarz* means."
Diane: "You know he told us that black means evil."

Recognizing the importance of his having to adjust his strategies as he got to know the students better, the German teacher, on the other hand, acknowledged that the learning process is a two-sided one. Adjusting his strategies, however, did not mean he had to abandon his goals. He stated:

Yes, yes because they are very individual . . . it's a learning process as much for me as it is for them. And I have to think about what my goals are, and my goals are really that they do the work I have planned, and that they learn German.

Negotiated Terrains of Expectation

Mr. Franklin's success with covering a great deal of material and with keeping the EXCEL students excited about learning German rested heavily on his ability to negotiate the terrains of expectation, that is, to devise strategies and to interact with them in such a way as to guide them toward taking responsibility, individually and as a group for their progress in class. By making frequent use of a game he devised and called "Jeopardy," for instance, he created an atmosphere in which his students learned to self-correct rather than simply waiting for him to answer, and they assisted each other in mastering various concepts. They volunteered freely during the games and commented frankly about who had or had not completed the work necessary to comprehend the activity or complete an assignment in class. By having the practice drills together or collaborate on dialogues, he appeared to relieve them of the anxiety brought on by individual recitation and at the same time succeeded in having them review or learn new material. While they appeared to have a tongue-in-cheek and sometimes sarcastic way of describing their positive regard for him, the data in the follow-up interviews reflect their enjoyment of the class and their high regard for his teaching methods. In the following example, after several minutes of working on an exercise where they are learning and practicing how to construct the superlative form of adjectives, two students express satisfaction about what they have accomplished during an exercise.

> Roger has tried to fill in a blank and asks, "Was I right?"(The teacher writes the correct answer on an overhead)
> Roger: "Yes, I was right!"
> Diana: "Hey, this is getting fun."

Because the students were instilled by the teacher with confidence about their ability to master various concepts and to compete successfully against students in schools with much older, larger, and well-established German programs, they, in turn, raised their expectations of themselves and became more vigorous participants in the learning process.

Teacher Standpoint on Achievement and Scholarship

Mr. Franklin, the German teacher, is a twenty-five-year-old European American who had taught introductory level German as a graduate student but had never taught high school level students. He was hired to teach German classes at Augustana for Project EXCEL students and any non-EXCEL students who wished to take language as an elective. His teaching supported him as he worked on a master's degree in German.

Mr. Franklin's insistence that his students take responsibility for their failures and their successes in the class sent a direct message about his high expectations of them as scholars. He chastised them for not having studied for a quiz but also reassured them that they were capable of performing well on any given test. He implicitly conveyed his expectations for achievement by giving them challenging assignments and by refusing to yield to protestations regarding tests and homework. Among the assignments on which they worked were essays in German on individually selected topics, e.g., pollution, violence, crime, cafeteria food, translation of part of the German constitution, the reading of a modern German play in preparation for a visit to see it performed (in English) on a university campus. The students, in turn, acknowledged his high standards and expressed their appreciation for the manner in which he maintained those standards. Some students noted:

> "I don't even think we need the books . . . he's doing a great job teaching us what he knows, writing on the board . . . discussing it, and doing the work."
> One student, Jeff, referred to the "high standards" of the German teacher, which he thought would "really get me ready for college."
> Another spoke of how the "challenging" English and German classes would "lead me into the future."

What We Learned

Emphasis on scholastic preparation without equal attention to a strong sense of academic identity ignores a significant factor in students' adjustment to college life (Allen, 1986; Fordham & Ogbu, 1986; Hernstein, 1994; Murray & Wexler, 1992; Vaz, 1987). The data from this phase of Project EXCEL underscore the need to continue research on the dynamics of social and cultural relations as well as the representations of "self" that exist in school settings. Further, they argue for investigations of the impact of such dynamics on the construction of a scholar identity as a central component of academic achievement. Finally, by focusing on the intersection of duality and standpoint in English and foreign language classrooms, this phase of the Project EXCEL study offers additional support for the kind of cross-curricula dialogues called for by researchers in education (Delpit, 1995; Giroux 1994; Jordan-Irvine, 1990). As Cosie (1997) reminds us:

> Those who would encourage academic success must, at the outset, acknowledge a harsh reality: that the line separating success from failure—intellectual life from death—can be tissue thin, especially in places where academic aspirations are more often stifled than encouraged. There are many graveyards for intellectual dreams in black and brown America, places where no one need read *The Bell Curve* to understand how little is expected of him or her, places where achievement is considered unnatural and discouragement lurks at every turn— often in the guise of sympathetic condescension from educators who, certain that most of their pupils will never be scholars, don't dare to challenge the Fates. Many black and brown children are still being told that academic accomplishment is so much beyond them that there is no real purpose in trying. They are receiving that message not only from the schools, but, in many cases, from virtually everyone around them. The very atmosphere, in large parts of America, is polluted with notions of intellectual inferiority (pp. 51–52).

For EXCEL students some classroom atmospheres offer dialogues that promote "notions of intellectual inferiority" that perpetuate savage inequalities, even for those African American students identified as college material. Chapter 4 offers two examples of the classroom atmospheres experienced by EXCEL students, examining the messages of achievement for them in the twelfth grade German and Advanced Placement English classes.

CHAPTER FOUR
Achievement Messages: Teacher/Student Dialogues in Twelfth Grade English and German Classes

In the preceding chapters, we have offered findings from our study of scholar identity development in educationally disadvantaged African American students and how that development did or did not impact academic achievement. The students were members of Project EXCEL, our longitudinal study of achievement motivation in African American and European American adolescents. For seven years, the project operated as a university-sponsored summer enrichment program focusing on reading, writing, and foreign language study, either French or German. Students participated in writing, reading, and foreign language activities that mirrored those presented in comparable first year and second-year university classes. When the project moved to Augustana High School, it became part of the regular college preparatory and Advanced Placement courses with the German class open to EXCEL and non-EXCEL students.

In this chapter we complete our report on the first EXCEL cohort based in a public high school. The participants joined the program as rising sophomores and at the time this chapter was written were graduating seniors. Previously, we presented findings based in part on in-class observations of teacher-student interactions. The analysis of these interactions suggests that performance expectations and the messages about how students are expected to meet them are embedded in the dialogues between teachers and students. This finding is not unique to EXCEL. Cummins (1986) argues that the social organization of the school and its bureaucratic constraints "reflect not only broader policy and societal factors but also the extent to which individual educators accept or challenge the social organization of the school in relation to minority students and their communities" (p. 10, as cited in Lipman, 1988, p. 23). "These relationships, in turn, reflect the ideology (whether formal theories or cultural models) of teachers who implement school policies, interact with children, make curricular choices, and so on" (Apple & Weis, 1983, as cited in Lipman, p. 26). Thus, teachers' ideological dispositions (a) influence how they define and label students and (b) affect their pedagogical choices. Everyday educational decisions reflect these ideologies in use, perceptions of students' strengths and weaknesses, and expectations for student performance and behavior (Keddie, 1971; as cited in Lipman, p. 26, 1991; Wilcox, 1982).

On the classroom level, how teachers interpret African American students' language, interactional styles, and competencies influences their assessments of these students' abilities (Michaels, 1981; Rist, 1970). These culturally inscribed interpretations, in turn, affect students' educational opportunities and assessments of their future role in society. Thus, student success or failure is constructed in the politics of everyday life in schools, in dynamic interactions between teachers, and students, and in the social organization of schools (McDermott, 1974 as cited in Lipman, 28).

In his book *Savage Inequalities* Kozol (1991) chronicles the systemic disparities in opportunity which perpetuate an educational caste system that results in academic genocide for poor children of all races in general and inner city children of color in particular. The invidious and insidious influence of master texts of inferiority in classrooms represents one form of this academic genocide that can affect identity construction and academic achievement. In recent years, educational researchers have offered theoretical perspectives on the political nature of the classroom as a means of better understanding the role of student-teacher interaction and the nature of these dialogues as they relate to identity construction (Apple, 1990; Cross, 1991) and cultural conflicts in the classroom (Delpit, 1995). In their dialogic exchanges with teachers, students not only negotiate the meaning of the subject being studied, but also they are forced, whether consciously or unconsciously, to reflect on themselves and constantly reposition and redefine themselves in light of the conflicting discourses they may encounter (Peck, 1992). If researchers and practitioners are to identify the factors that enhance as well as impede the academic progress of African American students, they must continue to examine how these students construct a sustaining academic identity and the relationship of that academic identity to achievement. Thus, cross-disciplinary studies that examine the power relations and political nature of the classroom can be useful to researchers and teachers across various fields (e.g., anthropology, applied linguistics, English, and English as a second language).

Gordon's (1995) study of the motivational patterns of resilient African American, high school sophomores supports the importance of self-concept in this population. Using a group of 138 urban students from impoverished and stressful backgrounds, Gordon investigated the relationship between self-concept and their "ability to thrive, mature, and increase competence in the face of adverse circumstances" (1993, p. 239), which she termed resilience. To determine resiliency status, socioeconomic status was determined using the Hollingshead Two Factor Index and stress by a self-report measure. Self-concept and motivation were measured by the High School Assessment of Academic Self-Concept and the Assessment of Personal Agency Beliefs. Two hypotheses guided the study. First, the resilient students and nonresilient students differ in their control and environmental support beliefs and in turn their self-concept and motivational patterns. Second, the resilient students and non-resilient students differ in their social beliefs as a dependent variable, not an independent variable (p. 245).

Gordon's findings on resilient students with respect to the cognitive domain are somewhat suggestive of our own findings about the importance of a scholar identity. Her findings propose that resilient students demonstrated a better cognitive self-concept and motivational pattern. Indeed, the resilient students distinguished themselves from the nonresilient students in all four dimensions of self-concept, not just the three that are associated with motivation (ability, environment, and importance). They possessed strong beliefs in their ability, as well as in their environment's support of their cognitive goals. Moreover, the results showed that these students also believed in their control over their cognitive goals and placed more emphasis on them than did their nonresilient counterparts. This made for a truly robust motivational pattern. The robust motivational pattern, in turn, made them firm in purpose and outlook, as well as able to overcome obstacles and endure stressors. As with the EXCEL students who developed scholar identities, the motivational pattern of the resilient students in Gordon's study differed from that of the nonresilient students.

Attention has also been directed toward the way cognitive constructs, such as perceptions of ability and control, interpersonal evaluation, future expectations and other inferences about why things occur, as well as personality factors, may affect achievement-related behavior in Blacks (Graham, 1989). Because self-esteem is prevalently construed to be a sub-set of the global self-concept and composed of "ideas and attitudes that are part of the self-evaluation process, one can develop and examine an academic self-concept in Black youth that will result in a model of self-efficacy and foster academic achievement" (Powell, 1989, p. 71). Powell suggests that this academic self-concept can also be enhanced by "pro-social strategies for coping with racism and overcoming the blocked opportunities that youngsters may encounter because of racism" (pp. 79-80).

In this chapter, we examine the dual messages about achievement conveyed to students through their experiences as individuals and as a group in their twelfth grade EXCEL English and German classes at Augustana. Eleven EXCEL students participated in the English class (September-December 1996). This was the third year of the project and through attrition, we had lost two of the original fourteen participants, one a Black male who had moved to another school in the area, and the second, a Black female who had joined several extracurricular activities which prevented her from scheduling EXCEL courses. Another student, a Black male, had been recommended for Basic rather than Advanced Placement English. There were also twelve other non-EXCEL students in the class, eight who were in the eleventh grade Advanced Placement class and four who had been in neither the tenth nor the eleventh grade Advanced Placement classes. All were African Americans while the teacher was a middle-aged European American male with eight years of teaching experience.

The class met from 8:30 to 10:00 a.m. during the first period in the first semester of block scheduling. As we noted in preceding chapters, all of the high schools in the city adopted this form of scheduling in which students had longer class periods for courses, but most of those courses lasted only one semester. All of the students' work (regardless of their previous Advanced Placement class experience) was evaluated using an Advanced Placement scale.

In the foreign language courses, six EXCEL students took German II/III and the remaining five took French II/III. The German teacher was the same European American male, in his mid-twenties, described in the previous chapter. The French teacher was a European-American female in her mid-twenties who was hired as a substitute because of the full-time teacher's maternity leave.

Methods, Data Collection, and Analyses

At the beginning and at the end of the academic year, EXCEL students and their teachers were interviewed by a trained interviewer not associated with the project. These interviews served two purposes:

1. To examine the congruence between classroom interaction themes and those emerging from participant interviews and
2. To document the development or non-development of scholar identity definitions in the student participants.

Teachers were also given the field notes to review for feedback and input into the interpretations of classroom interaction data.

We already had obtained permission from the German teacher for interviews with him and to conduct our observations. Prior to beginning the observations in the twelfth grade Advanced Placement English class, we met with the teacher, Mrs. Jones. At the meeting, we outlined the project and sought his permission to interview him and to observe the class. While reluctantly agreeing to the observations (Mr. Jones permitted only the observations because he was told to do so by the Assistant Principal), Mr. Jones refused to be interviewed (in the nine years of the project, Mr. Jones was the only teacher who was not interviewed). Although we assured Mr. Jones that the interview was intended to secure his perspectives on the Advanced Placement English class, he granted permission only for in-class observations and for the use of the interaction data collected. Therefore, we were unable to secure Mr. Jones' interpretations of interaction data or to have his input as we developed the themes that emerged from them. We consider those interpretations an important source of data for analysis, which was unavailable to us.

Since this portion of the study sought to understand what was occurring in the twelfth grade Advanced Placement class and in the foreign language classes, we chose to continue to use participant observation as the primary methodology. Specifically, we were interested in the meanings attached by students and the teachers. Parent interviews, the grades, writing samples, test scores, and school records, which were part of the larger study, were not primary sources for this phase. Instead, we emphasized observations of the students in English and in the German class, and interviews with the EXCEL students and the classroom teachers. Equivalent classroom data on non-EXCEL students were also collected. The absence of the full-time French teacher confined our discussion of student/teacher interactions to those occurring in the German class. The class continued during the spring semester with the same students from the previous semester.

Findings

Findings from both the English and German classes confirm the themes reported in the previous chapter that EXCEL students construct and reconstruct their identities based on their individual definitions of the meaning of scholar. Thus, these constructions centered on differing and sometimes conflicting messages, both direct and indirect, related to achievement and scholarship (Theme One). The duality of these messages, in turn, resulted in negotiated terrains of expectations which influenced students' behaviors and experiences in the classroom (Theme Two). Finally, the standpoints (Hill-Collins, 1990) of the teachers were revealed and expressed through direct and indirect messages on achievement and scholarship conveyed to students (Theme Three). The remainder of the chapter, drawn from this analysis, focuses on how each the three themes was enacted in the English and German classes.

Conflicting Messages Related to Achievement and Scholarship: The Twelfth Grade Advanced Placement English Class

During the English class, discussion centered on several required assignments, such as in and out of class readings, journal writing, vocabulary exercises, textbook work, essays and research activities, and analyses of major readings, including *Siddhartha, Heart of Darkness, Macbeth,* and *The Giver.* Other readings included poems and short stories connected with the celebration ("Awakening the Spirits") of a local Black artist, Bessie Harvey, whose work enjoyed a national and international reputation. Two conflicting messages were communicated strongly in the class:

1. The expectation that the students would produce in the Advanced Placement class at a level commensurate with their potential and at a level comparable to other Advanced Placement classes in the city, but the disbelief that they possessed the desire to do so; and
2. The teacher's assessment of the students' written work as superior to any he'd encountered previously at the school.

Mr. Jones often talked to the students about their preparedness for the course and for their future college courses. He emphasized attendance and called the roll by addressing each student as Mr. or Ms. and the student's last name. In a subsequent discussion of the field notes, Mr. Jones told the observer that he called the students by their last names to emphasize respect and formality. Despite this, on several occasions Mr. Jones commented on the poor class attendance of the students (11/14), the need for students and their parents to attend conferences (11/18), and his belief that the students were not putting enough effort into their assignments. His comments to students on several occasions supported this. Examples of their comments follow:

> You "don't see the necessity of spending enough time." (He insists that he'll) "turn it up . . . maybe I need to give you more." He warns them not to "come into my class asleep . . . (I) don't want to continue to wake you up in my class." He emphasizes, "I'm over it," and tells them he is going to "put you under enough of a workload" and that it has to be a "priority in life." "But you [must] take control and set your priorities, if you don't do it, you're going to pay. If you've got to spend four hours, I expect you to do that." He talks about not "fooling with this anymore."

In one instance explaining that he would not return papers because he had not yet recorded the grades, he commented:

> "I can tell you this, I am extremely disappointed . . . no one got the Halloween poem." Says that "it was, but it wasn't" about Halloween. "I want everybody to turn around. Not one person in here got it correct. The poem was about growin' old and dying."

By contrast, on more than one occasion, Mr. Jones told the students that they were the best group of writers he had:

> "Some of the essays were sloppy but some of the essays are among the best since I've been at Augustana. [You] are the best group of writers I've ever had. Overall, I want to say that I was surprised, I must say, pleasantly."

He talks about how happy he is with their papers because the students seem to be able to use new vocabulary.

> "Critical thinking and being able to read interpretively. I think that comes the more you read . . . mature is the word. I commend you. So far, it's wonderful."

In addition to these comments to students, Mr. Jones left a note for the substitute teacher stating that the class contained some of the best students he had ever taught.

Despite these positive messages, the students also received conflicting assessments of their work in comparison with other Advanced Placement classes in the city. For example, Mr. Jones noted in a discussion of the students' critical essay papers:

> "Show me what you can do . . . show me how well you . . . Show me your stuff." Victoria (one of the EXCEL students) says that her essay was about MoJo Farmer. The teacher agrees and adds, "You failed." He then follows up by telling the student that he has placed a large "X" on the paper and will take it to the East Tennessee English Teachers' meeting so that everybody can laugh at the student."

Although this comment is followed with the disclaimer, "No, I'm just kidding," in the context of similar comparisons, it underscores the conflicting messages that students received from Mr. Jones about their scholarship and achievement.

The Twelfth Grade German Class

In the German class the teacher placed emphasis on individual student needs. Because the class was small (seven in the Fall; and six in the Spring), he often was able to provide a great deal of attention to each student. Mr. Franklin used the overhead projector every day and, when the students were working individually, he moved around to give attention to each one and offered help and gradually gave less and less assistance as they mastered the material. During a reading exercise (they read in German and translated) the teacher said, "Okay. We'll start together and eventually you'll be on your own." Indeed, through the use of a variety of games, written exercises which focus on student interests, and activities requiring small group work, he got them to attend to the task at hand and seemingly stay involved.

As discussed in previous chapters, Mr. Franklin engaged the class using interactive games which required the students to use the German vocabulary and syntax they were acquiring. He also emphasized collaboration and teamwork in these exercises, so that students with more facility in the language could assist their classmates. During one game the following comment was overheard when a student coined a term in expressing her feelings about the subject:

> Melanie (to team mates): We got to think in German all right. We got to win this game.
> Another student, coining a word, referred to this as "thinking *deutschmatically*" [automatically in German].

In one observation session of the German class EXCEL student Jeff observed to Mr. Franklin:

> Jeff: Man, we need to extend German to the whole school.
> Teacher: Yeah, I agree with you.

The students encouraged each other to work hard, even to the point of sometimes chastising one another for not contributing to or working hard enough in group work or for looking at someone else's paper.

Mr. Franklin used a variety of methods to pressure the students' compliance, particularly on tasks on which they tended to procrastinate; this seemed to occur without any great effort on his part. It seemed that the students trusted in Mr. Franklin's expectation that they would succeed, an expectation which he expressed to the class and to the individual members of it. Thus, it appeared that the students were willing to work with him to complete required assignments, even when they expressed doubt about their complexity. Since Mr. Franklin also gave challenging tests, students also were concerned about their ability to do well. In one example, after a number of them had failed to complete an assignment, Mr. Franklin commented:

> Well, I think you guys are a little intimidated by this. And when I give you an assignment to do from it, you don't do it. Except for Felicia. I just think you guys don't think you can do it. But I want you to see that you can.

In another example, one student, worried about the extra credit assignment on an exam, expressed lack of confidence in his ability and the teacher reassured him:

> Roger: What's the point of taking this for extra credit? It's not going to make a difference.
> Teacher: Not true. You're still in this.

Frequent quizzes were used to develop vocabulary and to test concepts of grammar. When they read together, in class the teacher further reinforced familiar vocabulary by using it to teach them in the target language, words which they had not yet learned. The students responded well to this, and Mr. Franklin incorporated this technique more and more often as the year progressed.

The students were reminded—and generally seemed to recognize—that they had considerable talent, and the German teacher made it clear that he was very much committed to meeting their individual needs. In his interactions with them he was consistent about his high expectations, and the students as a result were motivated to excel. They continued to do so in the face of negative aspects of their classroom's surroundings and experiences in other classes which offered negative messages and conflicting discourses. There were constant interruptions from the intercom, teachers who came in and out of the classroom, and students selling items for fund-raising, since the class had to move from room to room during the second semester— hence, the frequent interruptions from teachers coming into their home room—and the interruptions were frequent and particularly disturbing. These negative aspects were to a great extent mitigated, however, by the teacher's strong positive messages. Students sometimes spoke about negative experiences in other classes. In one case a student in the German class complained about a rude math teacher who told her she was not capable of getting past the first chapter of the book. The student failed the math class, but she later passed it and did very well when she retook the course in the summer.

Recognizing the importance of his having to adjust his strategies as he got to know the students better, the German teacher, on the other hand, acknowledged that the learning process is a two-sided one. Adjusting his strategies, however, did not mean he had to abandon his goals. During his first year as a teacher at Augustana, he stated:

> Yes, yes because they (the students) are very individual . . . it's a learning process as much for me as it is for them. And I have to think about what my goals are, and my goals are really that they do the work I have planned, and that they learn German.

Duality of Messages Resulted in Negotiated Terrains of Expectations: The Twelfth Grade English Class

In the English class, the duality of messages regarding achievement and expectations continued throughout the semester. Throughout the observations, Mr. Jones' comments conveyed a duality in the messages, both in tone and substance (positive comments versus negative comments). He described himself as disappointed when no one interpreted a Halloween poem. Later, he described his comments as insulting and implied that he would not make them if he did not believe (the students) could do better. Despite this stated purpose, Mr. Jones used examples that could be interpreted by students as stereotypical.

In response to student comments that the book *Heart of Darkness* is racist, the teacher asserts that the book is not racist, but is simply human beings no matter what color their skin is. To this, one student (Alisha) says, "People thought we were evil (because of our skin color)." Mr. Jones follows up by saying that in the past blackness and evil were synonymous, that is, both were considered bad. "Now, that's racist." However, it was not about skin color, rather it was about the absence of light, since people lived in caves. "Darkness is associated with evil, bad, not slavery, not the American thing. Darkness is not racial, I want to make sure that you understand that; light has been associated with the truth. Does everyone understand?"

Later in the same lesson he asks: "How many of you are good people?" Several students raise their hands while others assert that they are "somewhere in between." Mr. Jones requests that students who think they are "bad" also raise their hands. "Why do you think you're a good person or a bad person?" "Write your rationale." He mentions the "black hat and white hat" as metaphors for "good" and "evil." Diana, one of the students, says, "It's color now." Mr. Jones responds, "No, it's not skin color." Mr. Jones also told the students that Augustana deserved its negative reputation in Clarksville. Students made brief comments and asked questions, but no one spoke out or disagreed with Mr. Jones' assertions. We need to point out that without the interview data from the teacher, it is not possible to assess Mr. Jones' intentions. Despite this, the observations suggest that students received dual messages regarding expectations which led to negotiations related to achievement throughout the semester.

The Twelfth Grade German Class

Mr. Franklin's success with covering a great deal of material and with keeping the EXCEL students excited about learning German rested heavily on his ability to negotiate the terrains of expectation, that is, to devise strategies and to interact with students in such a way as to guide them toward taking responsibility - individually and as a group - for their progress in class. By making frequent use of the game called Jeopardy, by offering challenging work on whether they worked collaboratively, and by consistently having them re-do work or do additional assignments for credit, he created an atmosphere in which his students learned to self-correct, rather than simply waiting for him to answer, and assist each other in mastering various concepts. They volunteered freely during the games, while demonstrating respect for one another as well as for the teacher, and commented frankly about who had or had not completed the work necessary to comprehend the activity or complete an assignment in class. By having them practice drills together or work cooperatively on dialogues, he addressed the sometimes anxiety occasioned by individual recitation and, at the same time, had them review or learn new material.

Because the students were instilled by the teacher with confidence about their ability to master various concepts and to compete successfully against students in schools with much older, larger, and well-established German programs and were motivated by his constant positive feedback and constructive criticism, these interviewers suggest that they raised their expectations of themselves and became more vigorous participants in the learning process.

Teacher Standpoint on Achievement and Scholarship

In both the English and German classes, teacher standpoint on achievement and scholarship were enacted for the students. As stated previously, Mr. Franklin, the German teacher, is a twenty-five-year-old European American who had taught introductory level German as a graduate student but had never taught high school level students. He was hired to teach German classes at Augustana for Project EXCEL students and any non-EXCEL students who wished to take language as an elective. His teaching supported him as he worked on a master's degree in German.

The description of Mr. Jones is based on informal conversations and observations of class sessions in which he gave autobiographical information. Mr. Jones grew up in Clarksville in a rural community. He attended high school in the area and then attended the state university in Clarksville where he majored in communications. After graduation, he continued to work at the university in film and video production for many years. He then decided to make a career change to become a teacher. Mr. Jones gained his certification to teacher and has been teaching at Augustana for seven or eight years. At the time of the study, he was the sponsor for the school newspaper and the yearbook. Mr. Jones also taught in an alternative program for high school students on week nights. He and his wife had two sons, ages eight and ten. Mr. Jones also had a grown daughter from a previous marriage who participated in Advanced Placement English classes in another local high school.

The Twelfth Grade English Teacher's Standpoint

Without interview data, Mr. Jones' standpoint is more difficult to validate. However, the observational data offer some contradictory insights.

Generally, when students were working in class, they were quiet. On occasion, Mr. Jones would ask students to stop talking when he was talking, giving an assignment, or allowing some time to work on assignments. On two occasions, once when discussing *Siddhartha* and another time when discussing an exercise on Poincaré's work (a type of exercise such as might be found on the ACT or SAT tests), students were asked to get in a circle. The students seemed more engaged in discussion with each other about *Siddhartha* than they had in the two years of previously observed English classes. However, in general, Mr. Jones felt that students needed to "solve their own problems" and did not involve them in any group work.

In several after-class conversations with the observer, Mr. Jones mentioned that he did not believe that the students were putting in enough effort on their work. His comments to students during the class supported this contention. As the semester progressed, Mr. Jones made fewer positive comments about the students' work. Despite these and earlier positive comments about the students' writing, failure and frustration appeared to be what Mr. Jones really expected from the students. During the class interactions in which Mr. Jones attempted to challenge or motivate the group or individuals through the use of "negative" comments, the students' non-response, despite their apparent discomfort, made it difficult to ascertain their response to Mr. Jones' attempts.

During class observations, over the weeks when *Heart of Darkness* was studied, tensions between Mr. Jones and the students regarding the symbolism found in the novel were obvious. Although Mr. Jones told the students that they could say anything they wanted to about the novel, in discussions about the symbolism associated with "the jungle," "white hats and black hats," and Kurtz' African mistress and European fiancée, the students' comments received little or no response. Thus, Mr. Jones' unwillingness to discuss the students' position, despite his call for deeper analysis of the book, appeared to deepen the students' resistance to participation, and so their perspectives on the symbolism and representation of black in the novel never surfaced.

In summary, although Mr. Jones stated that he expected the students in his Advanced Placement English class to perform at a high level, the duality of the messages related to achievement and scholarship resulted in constant negotiation and renegotiation of the classroom terrain. Particularly when the course content involved material which focused on race, Mr. Jones appeared unwilling to allow the students to discuss their perceptions of racist themes and, on some occasions, used their failure to perform at acceptable levels in his classroom as a confirmation of the weak academic reputation Augustana had in Clarksville. Thus, although the students in the Advanced Placement English class represented those with the highest grade point averages and the most potential to attend college, the messages regarding performance expectations were often contradictory. Moreover, Mr. Jones' comments in the German classes suggested appraisals of the students' potential that appeared analogous to the deficit models of Black achievement described in the literature (Lipman, 1998).

Importance of the Study

The data from this phase of Project EXCEL underscore the need to continue research on the dynamics of social and cultural relations, as well as the representations of self that exist in school settings. Further, they argue for investigations of the impact of such dynamics on the construction of a scholar identity as a central component of academic achievement. By the year 2010, thirty-eight percent of K-12 enrollment will be "minorities" and by 2020 forty-eight percent will be children of color (Carnegie Council on Adolescent Development, 1989). African Americans and Latinos already are a majority of the students in most large city school systems (Quality Education for Minorities, 1990, p. 15), and people of color are a majority in many urban areas. In the future, European-Americans will be a numerical minority in the United States, and the proportion of those who speak English as a first language will also decline. Clearly, the education of students of color and language minorities has serious implications for society as a whole (Lipman, 1998, p. 10). In examinations of the education of children of color in general, and African American children in particular, the relationship between identity construction and achievement continues to engage researchers' interest. African American disadvantaged students especially are even more acutely affected by variables which marginalize them and place them at the periphery of an educational system which, based on an "alleged meritocratic system" (Mickelson & Smith, 1992, p. 360), presumably aims to unilaterally support academic achievement. As Lipman (1998) notes:

> The meritocratic theory of academic success is an example of a commonly held cultural model that has significant implications for all students and for commonly held assumptions about social inequality. Its credibility rests on a set of implicit assumptions about equal opportunity, the rewards of hard work, and variation in human ability. But its explanatory power for the differential school success of students also rests with popularized stories and national myth about individuals who succeeded through hard work and superior talent. The myth resonates with personal stories of self-made success, which in turn confirms and nourishes the myth. Its concrete social power lies in its resonance with individuals who draw upon it to make sense of individual failure and success in school and to rationalize the failure of large numbers of students. Belief in meritocracy intersects with other cultural models and ideologies which assign more or less value to particular social groups, that is, races/ethnicities, genders, social classes, thus rationalizing an unequal social structure (p. 26).

Thus, disadvantaged students, burdened by schools inadequately equipped with materials and curricula that would better provide them with experiences routinely offered the best-prepared students, harbor an underdeveloped potential that remains neglected. Because of grade point averages that do not rank in the top ten percent, scores on standardized tests that do not exceed the national norm, and sometimes a lower economic status these students are prohibited from taking advantage of supplementary programs and materials to improve their skills. Despite this, they are often forced to adapt to an environment in which they are constantly entreated to achieve but in which they experience infrequent success and commonplace assaults on their competence. If the contradictory in-class messages we found in the EXCEL German and English classes impact definitions of achievement and the development of scholar identities, are such contradictory messages also found in the community where Augustana resides? The final chapter summarizes our findings from this cohort and discusses their possible implications for future studies of achievement among educationally disadvantaged African American high school students who possess the potential to succeed in college. We situate our presentation within the conceptual frameworks of Hudak and hooks.

CHAPTER FIVE
Undoing The Damage—Making Schools Work

In the previous chapters we have presented an overview of the activities of the third cohort of EXCEL students at Augustana High School. In exploring their in-class experiences with their teachers in English and German we have attempted to understand how these students construct their own scholar identities in the interactions with and through the expectations of their teachers. Our observations conducted over a three-year period lent additional support to the theories of several of our colleagues (Masten 1981; Spencer and Dornbush 1990; Hudak 1993; Ridley 1989; Ogbu 1988; hooks 1994; Anderson 1988; Peters 1988; Shade 1978; Taylor, Casten & Flickinger 1992), most particularly those who have examined resiliency issues, identity construction, and achievement among African American students.

In this chapter we want to offer some concluding data about EXCEL, as well as what we believe to be the implications of this research for others interested in studying the link between school context, identity construction, and achievement among the educationally disadvantaged African American students. We begin by providing an overview of the follow-up investigations of each cohort of EXCEL students.

PROJECT EXCEL FOLLOW-UP REPORT—MAY 1999

NAME	COHORT	INFORMATION
Student A	Cohort 1	After graduation from high school, this student left the area and we were unable to follow-up.
Student B	Cohort 1	Graduated from basic training at Ft. Benning, GA with a Certificate of Achievement for being selected an Honors Graduate of the cycle from Cycle No. 16-89. While stationed at Ft. Ord, Monterey, CA was nominated as Soldier of the Year. Also graduated from Air Assault School in CO. In 1/98 form indicated that he was attending UT and working at Federal Express as a courier.

continued on next page

NAME	COHORT	INFORMATION
Student C	Cohort 1	Currently employed at Lillian Vernon as Customer Communications and Data Entry Operator.
Student D	Cohort 1	Was a *Magna Cum Laude* graduate and a "Martin Luther King, Jr." scholar at Austin Peay University and was inducted into honoraries *Phi Beta Lambda* and *Gamma Beta Phi*; currently is a manager of an investment firm in Florida.
Student E	Cohort 1	Was employed at FBI as Investigative Communications Assistant. Received promotion in 1992 to position of Terminal Agency Coordinator for NCIC operations in the Clarksville office and received a Merit Award for work in hostage negotiators course. Met with then-FBI Director Williams Sessions. Was killed by a drunk driver while chaperoning children on a church related outing 10/93.
Student F	Cohort 1	At Tennessee State University, was named Who's Who Among Students in American Universities and Colleges, Dean's List, Phi Gamma Nu business fraternity, and was a *Cum Laude* graduate. Currently employed as Business Specialist for J.P. Morgan in Delaware, serving as liaison between Bank of New York and J.P. Morgan Private Banking of the firm. Volunteer for Ronald McDonald House and Red Cross as blood drive volunteer.
Student G	Cohort 1	Completed one year at TN Technological Institute. Enlisted in the Navy and was accepted into the Naval Nuclear Program, studying technical engineering. Is qualified to operate S5W, D2G, and A1W nuclear reactors on ships and submarines. Awarded the Navy Achievement Medal. Is now out of six-year enlistment obligation and looking for jobs. Hopes to obtain degree in mechanical engineering.
Student H	Cohort 1	U.S. Army, Bravo Team leader, Air Assault Weapons System Specialist. Served in Seoul, Korea as part of U.S. Embassy Guard Force. Also served as Instructor/Writer, U.S. Army and received many honors and special recognition awards, including Instructor of the Month (01/97). Is in the process of furthering education at Georgia Military College.

continued on next page

NAME	COHORT	INFORMATION
Student I	Cohort 1	Graduated from Roane State in 1991 and received A.A.S. degree in Nursing from Regents College in NY in 1992. Worked as registered nurse at a hospital in the southeast and is currently employed at Ft. Sanders Regional Medical Facility where chosen by a board of peers for Shift Leader in the Patricia Neal Rehab Center.
Student J	Cohort 1	Employed at Bank One in Atlanta GA.
Student K	Cohort 2	Graduated from University of Virginia with Master's in Counselor Education. Nominated for Cultural Fluency Award for participation in various multicultural programs and groups.
Student L	Cohort 2	Attended Pellissippi State Technical Community College. Did not complete degree.
Student M	Cohort 2	In management program with the Domino's Pizza company in a small town in Tennessee.
Student N	Cohort 2	Attended the University of Tennessee-Knoxville. Did not complete the degree.
Student O	Cohort 2	Employed at CenterPoint Detox & Rehabilitation Center for Adolescents (ages 13-18) as a alcohol and drug counselor in the Helen Ross McNabb Center.
Student P	Cohort 2	Attended University of Tennessee-Chattanooga and received UTC Freshman Scholarship.
Student Q	Cohort 2	Attending University of Tennessee-Knoxville.
Student R	Cohort 2	No data available after graduation from Ryan High School.
Student S	Cohort 2	Enrolled in Graduate School at University of Tennessee-Knoxville and completed first semester (Fall 98).
Student T	Cohort 2	Graduated with honors from Florida A&M University, May 1997 and currently working at Arthur Andersen L.P. in Houston, Texas.

continued on next page

NAME	COHORT	INFORMATION
Student U	Cohort 3	A sophomore at Pellissippi State Technical Community College this Fall, majoring in computer integrated drafting.
Student V	Cohort 3	Enrolled at Tennessee State University.
Student W	Cohort 3	Attending University of Tennessee-Knoxville.
Student X	Cohort 3	Currently attending Tennessee State University.
Student Y	Cohort 3	Completed first semester at Tennessee State University, GPA 3.8.
Student Z	Cohort 3	Attending the University of Memphis and holds a job there as a residence hall desk worker.
Student AA	Cohort 3	Currently attending Livingstone College in Salisbury, North Carolina.
Student BB	Cohort 3	Attending Pellissippi State Technical Community College Spring, 1999 and plans later to re-enter Tennessee State University.
Student CC	Cohort 3	Just completed first semester at Tennessee State University, GPA 2.75.
Student DD	Cohort 3	Made Dean's List at Tennessee State University and was still enrolled at the time of this follow-up.

Cohort 1 1989–1991
Cohort 2 1991–1994
Cohort 3 1994–1997

These follow-ups suggest that most of the EXCEL students engaged in activities which allowed them successfully to adapt either in college or in their careers despite the educational disadvantages, *ergo* average or below average ACT/SAT test scores, uneven study skills, and the mixed messages about achievement which they received from some of their teachers. Masten (1991) states that resilience in individuals refers to successful adaptation despite risk and adversity. Understanding resilience requires that obstacles to adaptation be understood and that the standard for or a definition of adapted behavior be delineated. For African American youngsters this resilience is connected with the issue of identity formation as Spencer and Dornbush (1990, see Boykin & Toms, 1985, for a discussion) noted:

For African-American youngsters, the issue of identity formation has added complexity due to the status of African Americans in U.S. society. Minority adolescents face the task of developing an identity in the context of a mainstream culture that views the attributes and values of minority groups as unfavorable. The decision making of African-American adolescents is further complicated because mainstream cultural values and African-American cultural traditions sometimes conflict (p. 120).

Therefore, the developmental task of achievement and social responsibility involves a need for such youngsters to evolve strategies for negotiating within their academic classrooms, particularly those classrooms in which their ability to succeed is questioned. For example, in Mr. Jones' twelfth grade English class the data suggest that EXCEL students received the message that they were not expected to meet the high standards required in a twelfth grade honors English class. At the same time, they were being exhorted to do their best and praised when their papers met that standard. In this regard, they faced each day Hudak's notion of "the ideal and the real." That is, the ideal twelfth grade honors student was presented to them as a goal to strive for at the same time they were confronting the real dilemma of the teacher's disbelief in their ability to achieve that goal. Hudak suggests that this tension between the real and the ideal causes adolescents who are marginalized to adopt "masquerading" as a survival skill and as a means to diffuse an otherwise racist situation. It is a balancing act in which some Black students engage because of the negative school experiences they have encountered. Racial discrimination is any behavior that systematically denies one group access to opportunities or privilege while perpetuating privilege for members of another group (Ridley, 1989). Racism is an ubiquitous social problem; its cause is hidden, but the result is known.

Oppositional Identity

According to Ridley (1989), institutional racism includes the intentional and unintentional manipulation or toleration of institutional policies that unfairly restrict the opportunities of targeted groups. Schools have great difficulty fulfilling Black students' need for self-esteem and their need to belong because in many ways they replicate the systemic racial discrimination found in the larger mainstream society. Social injustices, therefore, represent important sources of vulnerability for Black youth. As Ogbu (1988) has suggested, Black youth who are confronted with racism and respond with anger and rebelliousness may develop an oppositional social identity, that is, they may deliberately perform poorly in school, rebel against teachers and school administrators who are perceived as agents of oppression and shun any behavior associated with the mainstream society's expectations. Still other Black students may have a diffused identity characterized by low self-esteem and alienation from both the Black culture and the mainstream. Their poor academic and social competencies result in educational, social, emotional, and psychological adjustment problems. Therefore, although schools require a high degree of mainstream socialization from students, they do not always provide the environments conducive for Black students to acquire these skills while remaining connected to their home and community environments. For the EXCEL students who constructed scholar identities, such a mismatch between their homes and communities' expectations and those of the schools occasionally resulted in the kind of oppositional social identity suggested in Ogbu's work. The work of bell hooks is also illustrative in that she suggests that marginality itself can become a strategy, a technology in the construction of oneself, and the source of radical social action (hooks, as cited in Hudak, 1993 p. 174). Because Augustana High School had often been portrayed in the media as a context in which academic achievement was secondary to athletic ability, EXCEL students saw themselves as marginalized both within and outside of their school classrooms. In Chapter Two we relayed a conversation between the EXCEL students and their Tenth Grade Honors English Teacher, Ms. Young, about the different ways Augustana and its students were represented in Clarksville. This conversation illustrated Hudak's marginalized representation. In the course of the discussion, the students suggested that because Augustana was a "Black" school, its exposure in the media was disproportionately negative, with the inference that "bad kids," i.e., those who were frequently involved with the juvenile justice system, were the ones who matriculated at Augustana. Moreover, because of this perceived population, there was a tendency to expect the worst from the students.

The students also recognized that the school was mainly considered a sports academy recognized for the success of its football and basketball teams. However, students also noted that this image was partially the result of apathy on the part of the students toward academic excellence. For example, they expressed frustration with how little had been accomplished by the class officers they had elected. They also blamed sponsors who did not facilitate the kind of activist agenda they felt was needed to change Augustana's image with internal and external constituencies.

Miss Young also suggested in a follow-up interview that the image of Augustana within the larger community was tied to "violence and ignorance." She recounted how her teaching at Augustana often elicited sympathy from teacher colleagues at other schools. Moreover, she believed the Clarksville community felt that academically adept students were not found at Augustana, but rather students who required remedial attention. As she stated in the interview:

> "And it really bothers me. It bothers me number one because we've got some very bright, bright kids here. I hate for them to be perceived that way, and I feel that a lot of the kids perceive themselves that way because of that kind of pressure. The more we're out in the community, the more we participate in academic contests instead of just sports contests, the more we make a name for ourselves and a good name [the better our image will be]. You know if I could do anything single-handedly, if I could do that, you know, we could go out in speech contests and things of that nature and make a name for ourselves and people [would] say, "Oh, my gosh, there's somebody from Augustana, you gotta be good."

Ms. Young's comments, as well as those of the EXCEL students. Suggest an awareness of the community's low expectations and the barrier those expectations pose for students who seriously engage in academic pursuits at Augustana. Our findings underscore those other studies which suggest a link between student perception and academic achievement among Black adolescents.

Responses to Marginality

A number of these researchers have also looked at adolescents' reactions to their experiences and awareness of marginality. For example, Anderson (1990) discussed the social experiences and behavior of African-American males as they cross into and out of two inner-city communities, one an economically disadvantaged African-American community, the other an integrated community experiencing gentrification. Anderson's analysis clearly reveals that adolescents' behavior is shaped by the nature of the environment they inhabit, and by their perceptions of how they are viewed (e.g., with fear, suspicion, or apprehension) by those with whom they interact. Anderson suggested that the affect of the social environment and the strategies of negotiation the adolescents use affects Black adolescents' ability to view themselves as useful participating members of society. Ogbu suggested that as a consequence of their perception that racial discrimination limits their social mobility; African-American adolescents are more likely to reflect White middle-class values and attitudes in the area of education. School learning is viewed as a subtractive process with few identifiable benefits, in which individuals must sacrifice something of their collective sense of identity in adopting the behaviors and values favored in school.

Ogbu (1988) also argued that as a consequence of their awareness of and experiences with racial barriers to conventional means of achieving social mobility, African Americans in inner cities have responded by developing alternative theories and strategies for achieving social and economic success. According to this view, although inner-city African-American parents stress the importance of formal education and conventional jobs, they also consciously or unconsciously teach their children the value of "instrumental competencies of clientship, hustling or other survival strategies" (p. 57).

The experiences and perceptions of adolescents and their family members regarding racial discrimination and racial barriers may directly influence the conscious and unconscious commitment of parents and adolescents to the adolescents' schooling and to the assumption of mainstream values and behaviors. Further, the adolescent categories discussed by Ogbu represent ways in which adolescents may rationalize their identity and self-concept. They represent sets of values, attitudes, and behaviors that African-American adolescents may adopt to help guide them in decision making in critical areas such as schooling and peer relations.

Peters (1988) asserted that African-American parents may actively socialize their children to prepare for encounters with racial discrimination. Peters suggested that African-American parents often seek to inoculate their children against discriminatory mistreatment by promoting the self-esteem and self-confidence of their children and by stressing the importance of school achievement. Bowman and Howard (1985) obtained data showing that to the extent that African-American parents discuss with their adolescents the nature of race-related barriers to social mobility, the youngsters perform better in school. These results also offer insight into the factors and processes that promote resilience in African-American adolescents. These factors are what Masten (1981) describes as protective factors, and they appear to moderate the effects of risk factors on adolescent development.

Shade (1978) argued that social science has been able to alleviate any social guilt that might be generated by placing the blame for their academic difficulties on Blacks themselves. Specifically, apologists for current educational practices ground their conclusions in stigma theory, enabling them to define the problem in terms of bored, unmotivated, and apathetic children influenced by a less than adequate home environment.

Parental Support Academic Achievement:
Findings Discussed Earlier in This Chapter

Our EXCEL data supported the research found above. We found that the parents of our participants strongly supported academic excellence and achievement for their children. Indeed across socio-economic groups both middle income and low income parents of our participants wanted their children to experience academic success and building on that success to go to college. They expressed concern about the hidden messages of inferiority given to their children across their school lives and saw enrichment programs like EXCEL as one way to diffuse these messages. These findings support those of other researchers (e.g., Taylor, Casten, & Flickinger, in press; Taylor & Roberts, 1992) who suggest that the factors responsible for adolescents' adjustments were their parenting experiences and kinship social support. As with our EXCEL students, these researchers found that the strong parental support influenced greatly the achievement motivation of their children. Thus, strong parental support, academic preparation, and an understanding of the systemic barriers to achievement faced by African American adolescents in schools were all findings suggested by our data. Yet our data also raised issues and questions for future investigation.

In the second edition of her book, *Affirming Diversity: The Sociopolitical Context of Multicultural Education,* Nieto (1996) suggests that reviewing the transcripts and interviews of her participants had caused her and her associates to think more carefully about the meaning of success for these students (p. 17). This reflection produced the following list of conditions in order for a student to be considered successful:

- They were still in school and planning to complete high school, or at least recently graduated.
- They had good grades, although they were not necessarily at or near the top of the class.
- They had thought about the future and made some plans for it.
- They generally enjoyed school and felt engaged in it.
- They were critical of their own school experiences and those of peers.
- Most important, they described themselves as successful (p. 18).

Applying Nieto's conceptual framework to our own study, the students who participated in all three cohorts of EXCEL could be considered successful. All of them graduated from high school and attained the necessary grades to do so. A major criterion for EXCEL involved the desire to go to college and a minimum GPA of 2.5 when the student entered the program. Through a written application, students self-selected into EXCEL. In addition to demographic and transcript information, students were asked to write about their future college aspirations as well as their reasons for wanting to be considered for EXCEL.

Over the three-year period (Cohort #3), in classroom observations and interviews, we learned that the students enjoyed their school experiences and had no difficulty identifying and critiquing the systemic school and community barriers they believed contributed to ineffective instruction in their classes. In the 10th grade English class and particularly in their observations of instruction in their 12th grade AP English class, they described their school experiences and how those experiences affected their perception of teacher expectations relative to their own achievement.

For example, as we noted in an earlier chapter, despite the positive messages about their scholarship and the expectation of high achievement, the EXCEL students were well aware of the largely negative community perception of their school and its effects on academic resources:

"Shipley, Holt, Sharp and Thompson (other schools in the community with low black enrollments) get publicity that tends to be positive. (When they talk about Augustana), they mention shooting and fighting."

"They put less money in black schools" (one student remarked during a discussion of the newspaper article comparing Augustana with its peer school). We have a new gym but other parts of the building are crumbling.

"The families in Shipley, Holt, Sharp and Thompson have more money and get more done in their schools than people in this school."

Most importantly, like Nieto's participants, those who developed scholar identity, and some who did not, described themselves as successful:

"[Being a scholar means] a mature way of looking at things like schoolwork-like you have to be on top of your schoolwork, pay attention in class, be respectful to teachers and classmates...A professional type attitude."

Students also mentioned leadership ability, attitude and self-respect. For other students the ability to do well academically was a major factor while for others, just doing the best they were capable of, and having a "stick to it attitude" were sufficient indicators.

Nieto also points out that the students in her study felt that they were entitled to an education, and that they were eager to talk about problems with the school. They had little difficulty critiquing the school or offering suggestions about how to make the experience more effective, whether or not they considered themselves to be successful in school.

In the follow-up interviews conducted one year after graduation from high school, all of the EXCEL students offered suggestions about how their school experiences could have better prepared them for either college or the world of work. In most cases these discussions centered on the inadequate academic preparation they had received in high school (e.g., insufficient mathematics and science course offerings).

Research Findings/Ethical Dilemmas

Moreover, although students who developed a scholar identity and articulated a definition were more likely to describe themselves as successful, even those who were experiencing difficulty in their first year of college or in a training program did not frame that difficulty in terms of lack of success.

By focusing on scholar identity we hoped to understand how it might contribute to academic achievement in our participants. This meant that while some of our participants did not develop scholar identity, those who did tended to complete college, military or job training. Although we are not suggesting a causal relationship between scholar identity and achievement, we do believe that explorations of variables which might contribute to school success can be useful in "understanding the conditions for success that families, schools, and communities together can provide" (Nieto, 1996, p. 19).

Moreover, we agree with Nieto and others that too much research has tended to focus on the academic failure of African American students (Thernstrom & Thernstrom, 1997). As Smith, Gilmore, Goodman, & McDermott (1993 as cited in Nieto, 1996) suggest, "failure of failure" has been characterized thus:

> Once the threat of failure and the pressures of success are pushed aside, once we recognize that the task of schooling is not to explain which students do or do not learn, learning becomes easy for most. This will require the dismantling of the elaborate apparatus we have erected for documenting the failures of our children and redirecting the energies taken by that enterprise into organizing more learning. We must instead confront the very idea of school failure, seeing it for what it is, manifestations of classism and racism (p. 19).

Thus, although our study may provide some insight into the role of scholar identity in academic achievement, we are concerned that in focusing on success alone, we may be inadvertently contributing to a body of literature which either "blames the victim" (e.g., the students who do not succeed academically) or worse attributes racist or classist motives to teachers (e.g., possible perceptions of the 12th grade AP English teacher in our study) when they may not be present. Instead, we believe that there is much to be learned from students who do not succeed in school and an issue for us is the possibility that our research will inadvertently support policies which make academically unsuccessful students "casualties of educational systems that cannot 'see' them because their problems remain invisible" (Nieto, 1996 p. 19).

Acting White

Fordham and Ogbu (1986) suggest that the academically successful students in Capital High masked their ability to do well because they did not wish to be accused of "acting white." "Acting white" in this study was equated with valuing educational excellence by those African American students who amassed modest academic records or who were failing.

Equating academic success with "acting white" did not emerge as a theme in our research. Over the course of 10 years, and the three cohorts of students we studied, some developed scholar identities, while others did not. However, of those students who defined themselves as scholars, none suggested that they viewed academic success as a betrayal of their racial or ethnic identities.

Moreover, even those EXCEL students who did not remain in or complete college did not give "acting white" as the reason they left college or failed the majority of their first-year required courses. Instead, these students talked about inadequate high school preparation in mathematics and science, the lack of financial resources and poor study and time management skills as contributing factors. None of these relate to the category "acting white" as defined in Fordham & Ogbu's research.

Building Effective Educational Contexts

How then do we provide effective educational experiences and contexts for educationally disadvantaged African American students?

The research of Jordan Irvine (1990) provides some insights. Her work focuses on how teacher expectations influence the achievement of children in general and African American children in particular. In her book *Black Students and School Failure: Policies, practices, and prescriptions,* she cites the four-factor theory of teacher expectation developed by Rosenthal (1974 as cited in Cooper, 1985) which offers the following positive aspects of teacher expectation:

1. Climate: Teachers should create warm socioemotional relation-ships with students. Teachers more often create these types of climates with their brighter students.

2. Feedback: Teachers should provide feedback to students about their performance. Teachers tend to praise high-expectation students and criticize low-expectation students.
3. Input: Teachers should teach quantitatively more material and qualitatively more challenging material. Students perceived as low-expectation receive fewer opportunities to learn and are taught less difficult material.
4. Out put: Teachers should give students more opportunities to respond and ask questions. Teachers give preferential treatment by giving high-expectation students more clues, longer response times, and with more repeats, redirects, and rephrases (pp. 44-45).

Cooper (1985, as cited in Jordan-Irvine, 1990) suggests that classroom climate can be directly influenced by teachers' perceptions of the amount of control they exercise over in-class interactions (particularly those between themselves and the student). Moreover, the amount of perceived control is also related to whether the setting is public or private. Regardless of the setting or who initiates the interaction, students for whom the teacher holds high expectations will succeed. On the other hand, Cooper's model suggests that low-expectation students succeed when teacher control is high, student initiations are few, and the interactions with teachers occur in private rather than publically. The model also discusses the role students' self-efficacy beliefs play in teacher expectations. It suggests that teacher expectations are high for those students who complete academic work successfully and who do so because they believe that they can achieve mastery without much teacher assistance.

Jordan-Irvine (1990) also notes that teachers socialize and condition student academic behavior through both the hidden and stated curriculum. "They consciously and unconsciously inculcate students for their appropriate role in the institution by delivering messages, sanctions, and rewards about appropriate behavior and expectations."

The teacher/student relationship exerts such a powerful influence because it resembles that of parent/child. Indeed, Jackson (1983, as cited in Jordan-Irvine, 1990) agrees, estimating that from the time a child enters kindergarten until that same child enters middle school, he/she spends more than seven thousand hours in school. Thus, from the age of six onward this student is more familiar to his/her teacher than to his/her father and possibly even his mother. Further, Jackson's work suggests that teacher warmth, affect, and enthusiasm are important attributes, highly correlating with student achievement (pp. 44-48).

Indeed, as Johnson and Prom-Johnson (1986, as cited in Jordan Irvine, 1990) concluded, "It appears that while talented students are strongly influenced toward growth and development during the school years, the way in which this happens is through the interpersonal skills and affective characteristics of good teachers" (p. 279).

In related work, Shade, B., Kelly, C., & Oberg, M. (1997) describe how to create culturally responsive classrooms for students of color (i.e., African American, American Indian, Mexican American and Hmong). Their guide focuses on helping teachers to understand student differences from an environmental and contextual perspective, explaining how to engage students in the learning process so that they can increase their academic performance. These authors provide strategies, references and culturally-related information intended to assist teachers in recognizing how cultural differences influence learning and how to make use of those differences to build effective learning environments for their students. A great deal of attention is given to the effect of teacher affect on student performance and success.

While acknowledging the role of teacher affect and interaction on African American student achievement, Jordan-Irvine (1990) also points out that these children have difficulty mediating teachers' negative expectations because of their race, class, family background, perceptions of their skin color as unattractive, the behavior of their siblings, and their often unusual names. Racism, discrimination, and the general devaluation of black people and their culture have also limited black children's development of a healthy sense of self, high expectations, and inner-directed orientations (1990, p. 53).

This "guilt by association" implies that black students must demonstrate to teachers that the negative stereotypes generally associated with black students' behavior do not pertain to them. This imposed denial and refutation of one's cultural heritage and racial identity are directly related to black self-hatred, lowered self-esteem, and heightened anxiety and possibly to lower academic achievement (p. 56).

Three years of observing EXCEL students in English and German classes supported the work on Jordan Irvine and others regarding teacher/student interactions and the influence such interactions had on student achievement, particularly in the German class. However, while our data substantiated the findings of the researchers we've cited, they did not provide definitive strategies for establishing a classroom in which students could construct definitions of scholar and scholarship positively correlated to achievement. For us and others interested in providing positive environments in which to counteract the hidden curriculum as well as mediate some teachers' negative expectations of black children's academic ability, the issue remains a research conundrum.

Future Research Directions

The work of Cosie (1997) and Freire (1970), as well as new statistics on Black college graduation rates, offer interesting directions for future research.

In his newest book, *Color-blind (Seeing Beyond Race in a Race-Obsessed World)*, Cosie (1997) describes three universities who have achieved notable African American admission, retention and graduation rates. After a lengthy discussion of the programs in each of these institutions, he concludes by offering the following possible explanation for their success:

> Neither the faculty of Xavier University and Georgia Tech nor Tresiman discovered something magical, and there is nothing about their methods that is difficult to understand. Their approach can be reduced to six simple steps (1) find a group of young people motivated to learn or find a way to motivate them; (2) convince them you believe in them; (3) teach them good study skills, including the art of studying in groups; (4) challenge them with difficult and practical material; (5) give them adequate support; and (6) demand that they perform. And, lo and behold, they do (Cosie, 1997, p. 65).

Paulo Freire (1970) suggests that educational institutions and the teachers within in them engage in what he terms "banking education" in which students become nothing more than repositories for the knowledge, skills, behaviors and attitudes of the teachers and administrators with whom they work. Moreover, the curriculum from which the knowledge, skills, and behaviors derived replicates the culture of power and oppressions of society at large. Thus, instead of using the knowledge and skills acquired in class, dialogues and fieldwork in their own communities to develop strategies for attacking and ultimately dismantling systemic oppression, students are asked to "bank" information for regurgitation on tests or in class-related projects. Freire notes that such education does not prepare individuals to develop alternative solutions to important societal problems. Nor does it provide opportunities for practicing the kind of "thinking outside the box" required to develop such alternatives.

A Place to End and Begin

Focusing on the graduation rates of educationally disadvantaged students is particularly important to educators and researchers interested in constructing effective learning contexts. The graduation rates for African American students was reported in a recent issue of the *Journal of Blacks in Higher Education*; in this issue (Winter 2000/2001, Number 30), the new Census Bureau statistics on blacks with college educations were cited. The researchers found that these individuals on average earn incomes that were double the incomes of blacks with only a high school diploma. Even more impressive was the fact that blacks with a college degree have a median income that is 89 percent of the median income of whites with a college degree.

However, all of this good news was marred by the fact that statistics also show that only 15 percent of all adult African Americans now hold a college degree. This raises the question, why aren't more blacks graduating from college? (p. 90).

After ten years of longitudinal research with three cohorts of EXCEL students, we suggest that K-12 experiences which provide academically challenging work, appropriate study skills and the presentation of content within a context of culturally relevant pedagogy represent important strategies to investigate for those interested in the achievement of educationally disadvantaged students of color. While we recognize that we join other researchers in calling for these investigations, our findings suggested that for EXCEL students expecting excellence extended their learning. Perhaps for those of us who want to promote academic excellence, this expectation, while obvious, may be the place to begin.

REFERENCES

Allen, W. (1986). *Gender and race differences in black student academic performance, racial attitudes and college satisfaction.* Atlanta, GA: Southern Educational Foundation. (ERIC Document Reproduction Service No. ED 268 855).

Andersen, M. L., & Collins, P. H. (1992). Preface in M.L. Andersen & P. H. Collins (Eds.), Race, *class, and gender: An anthology* (pp. xii-xvi). Belmont, CA: Wadsworth.

Anderson, E. (1990). *Streetwise: Race, class, and change in an urban community.* Chicago: University of Chicago Press.

Apple, M. W. (1993). Constructing the "other": Rightist reconstructions of common sense. In C. McCarthy & W. Crichlow (Eds.), *Race, identity and representation in education* (pp. 24-39). New York: Routledge. (1990). *Ideology and curriculum* (2nd ed.). New York: Routledge.

Atkinson, J. W. (1966). *A theory of achievement motivation.* New York: Wiley.

Boykin, A. W., & Toms, F. D. (1985). Black child socialization: A conceptual framework. In H. McAdoo & J. McAdoo (Eds.), *Black children: Social, educational, and parental environments* (pp. 33-51). Newbury Park, CA: Sage

Bowman, P. J., & Howard, C. S. (1985). Race-related socialization, motivation and academic achievement: A study of black youth in three-generation families. *Journal of Academy of Child Psychiatry, 24,* 134-141.

Carnegie Council on Adolescent Development. (1989). *Turning points: Preparing American youth for the 21st century.* New York: Carnegie Corporation.

Castenell, L. N., Jr., & Piner, W. F. (1993). (Eds.). *Understanding curriculum as racial text: Representations of identity and difference in education.* New York: SUNY.

Castenell, L. (1984). A cross-cultural look at achievement motivation research. *Journal of Negro Education, 53(4)*, (pp. 435-443).

Collins, R. L. (1993). Responding to cultural diversity in our schools. In C. McCarthy & W. Crichlow (Eds.), *Race, identity and representation in education* (pp. 115-208). New York: Routledge.

Cosie, E. (1997). *Color-blind: Seeing beyond race in a race-obsessed world.* New York: Harper Collins.

Cummins, J. (1986). Empowering minority students: A framework for intervention. *Harvard Educational Review, 56* (1), (pp. 18-36).

Cross, W. E., Jr. (1991). *Shades of black: Diversity in African-American identity.* Philadelphia: Temple University.

Delpit, L. (1995). *Other people's children: Cultural conflict in the classroom.* New York: New Press.

Edwards, A., and Polite, C. K. (1992). *Children of the dream: The psychology of black success.* New York: Doubleday.

Ferguson, R. F., (1993). Outcomes of mentoring: Healthy identities for youth. *Journal of Emotional and Behavior Problems V3, N2,* (pp. 19-22) Summer 1994.

Fine, M. (1994). Working the hyphen: Reinventing self and other. In N. K. Denzen & Y. S. Lincoln (Eds.), *Handbook of Qualitative Research* (pp. 70-82). Newbury Park, CA: Sage.

Fordham, S. (1988). Racelessness as a factor in black students' school success: Pragmatic strategy or pyrrhic victory? *Harvard Educational Review, 58 (1),* (pp. 54-84).

Fordham, S., & Ogbu, J. (1986). Black student's school success: Coping with the burden of acting white. *Urban Review, 18 (3),* (pp. 176-206).

Foucault, M. (1988). The ethic of care for the self as a practice of freedom. In J. Bernauer & D. Rasamussen (Eds.), *The final Foucault.* Cambridge: Massachusetts Institute of Technology.

Freire, P. (1970). *Pedagogy of the oppressed.* (M. B. Ramos, Trans.). New York: Seabury. (Original manuscript published 1968).

Giroux, Henry A. (1994). *Between Borders: Pedagogy and the politics of cultural studies.* New York: Routledge.

Goetz, J. P., & LeCompte, M. D. (1984). *Ethnography and qualitative design in educational research.* New York: Academic Press.

Gordon, K. A. (1995). Self-concept and motivational patterns of resilient African American high school students. *Journal of Black Psychology, 21(3),* (pp. 239-255).

Graham, S. (1989). Motivation in Afro-Americans. In G. Berry and J. Assannen (Eds.), *Black students: Psychosocial issues and academic achievement* (pp. 40-68). Newbury Park, CA: Sage.

Hall, S. (1992). Cultural studies and its theoretical legacies. In Grossberg, Nelson, & Treichler (Eds.), *Cultural studies* (pp. 227-294). New York: Routledge.

Hatch, J. A. (1985, June). *Naturalistic methods in educational research.* Paper presented at the meeting of the *Centro Interdisciplinario de Investigacion y Docencia en Educacion Tecnica,* Queretaro, Qro. Mexico.

Hill-Collins, P. (1990). *Black feminist thought: Knowledge, consciousness, and the politics of empowerment.* New York: Routledge, Chapman and Hall, Inc.

hooks, b. (1994). *Teaching to transgress: Education as the practice of freedom.* New York: Routledge.

Hudak, G. M. (1993). Technologies of marginality: Strategies of stardom and displacement in adolescent life. In C. McCarthy and W. Crichlow (Eds.), *Race, identity, and representation in education* (pp. 172-187). New York: Routledge.

Jordan Irvine, J. (1990). *Black students and school failure: Policies, practices, and prescriptions.* New York: Greenwood.

The Journal of Blacks in Higher Education (p. 46), Summer 1999. New York: CH II PUBLISHERS, INC.

The Journal of Blacks in Higher Education (p. 90), Winter 2000/2001. New York: CH II PUBLISHERS, INC.

98

Kaplan, A. (1964). *The conduct of inquiry.* San Francisco: Chandler.

Kozol, J. (1991). *Saving inequalities.* New York: Crown Publishing, Inc.

LeCompte, M., & Preissle, J. (1993). *Ethnography and qualitative design in educational research* (2nd ed.). San Diego: Academic Press.

Lipman, P. (1988). *Race, class, and power in school restructuring.* New York: SUNY.

Lorde, A. (1984). *Sister outsider: Essays and speeches.* Freedom, CA: Crossing.

Maehr, M. (1974). Culture and achievement motivation. *American Psychologist, 29,* (pp. 887-896).

Masten, A. S. (1989). Resilience in development: Implications of the study of successful adaptation for developmental psychopathology. In D. Cicchetti (Ed.). *The emergence of a discipline: Rochester symposium on developmental psychopathology* (Vol 1, pp. 261-294) Hillsdale, NJ: Lawrence Erlbaum Associates.

McCarthy, C. (1990). *Race and curriculum.* London: Falmer.

McCarthy, C., & Crichlow, W. (1993). Introduction: Theories of identity, theories of representation, theories of race. In C. McCarthy and W. Crichlow (Eds.), *Race, identity, and representation in education* (pp. xiii-xxix). New York: Routledge.

McClelland, D.C. (1953). *The achievement motive.* New York: Appleton-Century-Crofts.

McIntosh, P. (1992). White privilege and male privilege: A personal account of coming to see correspondences through work in women's studies. in M. L. Andersen & P. H. Collins (Eds.), *Race, class, and gender: An anthology* (pp. 359-376). Belmont, CA: Wadsworth.

Merriam, S. B. (1988). *Cast study research in education: A qualitative approach.* San Francisco: Jossey-Boss.

Michaels, S. (1981). Sharing time: Children's narrative styles and differential access to literacy. *Language Socialization, 10,* (pp. 423-442).

Mickelson, R. A., & Smith, S. S. (1992). Education and the struggle against race, class, and gender inequality. In M. L. Andersen & P. H. Collins (Eds.), *Race, class, and gender: An anthology* (pp. 359-376). Belmont, CA: Wadsworth.

Murray, C., & Hernstein, R. (1994). *The bell curve: Intelligence and class structure in American life.* New York: Free Press.

Nieto, S. (1992). *Affirming Diversity: The sociopolitical context of multicultural education.* New York: Longman Publishers USA (1994). Lessons from students on creating a chance to dream. *Harvard Educational Review, 64 (4),* (pp. 392-426).

Oakes, J (1985). *Keeping Track: How schools structure inequality.* New Haven: Yale University.

Ogbu, J. (1978). *Minority education and caste: The American system in cross-cultural perspective.* New York: Academic Press. (1988). Class stratification, race stratification, and schooling. In L. Weis (ed.), *Class, Race and gender in American education.* Albany: State U of New York.

Omi, M., & Winant, H. (1994). *Racial formation in the United States: From the 1960's to the 1990's* (2nd ed.). New York: Routledge.

Peters, M. (1988). Parenting in black families with young children: A historical perspective. In H. McAdoo (Eds.), *Black families.* Newbury Park, CA: Sage.

Powell, G. J. (1989). Defining self-concept as a dimension of academic achievement for inner-city youth. In G. Berry and J. Assannen (Eds.), *Black students: Psychosocial issues and academic achievement* (pp. 69-82). Newbury Park, CA: Sage.

Quality Education for Minorities Project. (1990). *Education that works: An action plan for the education of minorities* (p. 15). Cambridge, MA: Author, Massachusetts Institute of Technology.

Ridley, C. R. (1989). Racism in counseling as an adverse behavioral process. In P. B. Pedersen, J. G. Draguns, W. J. Lonner, & J. E. Trimble (Eds.), *Counseling across cultures* (3rd ed.). Honolulu, HI: University of Hawaii Press.

Rist, R. (1970). Student social class and teacher expectations: The self-fulfilling prophecy in ghetto education. *Harvard Educational Review, 40*, (pp. 411-451).

Shade, B., Kelly, C., & Oberg, M. (1997). *Creating culturally responsive classrooms.* Washington D.C.: American Psychological Association.

Shade, B., & Robinson, J. (1997). *Culture, Style and the educative process: Making schools work for racially diverse students* (2nd ed.). Springfield, IL: Charles C. Thomas Publisher, Ltd.

Spencer, M. B. & Dornbush, S. M. (1990). Challenges in studying minority youth. In S. Feldman & G. Elliott (Eds.), *At the threshold: The developing adolescent* (pp. 123-146). Cambridge, MA: Harvard University Press.

Taylor, R. D., Casten, R., & Flickinger, S. (1992). *Explaining the school achievement of African-American adolescents.* Manuscript submitted for publication.

Thernstrom, S. & Thernstrom, A. (1997). Skills, Tests, and Diversity. *American in black and white one nation, indivisible: Rage in Modern America* (p. 352). New York: Simon & Schuster

U.S. Department of Education National Center for Education Statistics (1996). *The condition of education, 1996* (NCES 96-304). Washington, DC: Author.

Vaz, K. (1987). Building retention systems for talented minority students attending white universities. *Negro Educational Review, 38 (1)*, (pp. 26-29).

Welch, O. M., Hodges, C.R., and Warden, K. (1989). Developing the scholar ethos in minority college-bound students: The vital link. *Urban Education, 24 (1)*, (pp.59-76). (1997). *Standing outside on the inside: Black adolescents and the construction of academic identity.* New York: SUNY.

Wexler, P. (1992). *Becoming somebody: Toward a social psychology of school,* (p. 9). Washington, D.C.: Falmer.

White, J. L., & Parham, T. A. (1970). *The psychology of blacks: An African-American perspective.* Englewood Cliffs: Prentice-Hall.

White, J. L. (1984). *The psychology of blacks: An Afro-American perspective.* (2nd ed.), Englewood Cliffs: Prentice-Hall.

Yin, P. K. (1989). *Case study research.* Newbury Park, CA: Sage.

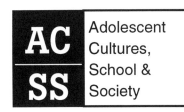

Joseph L. DeVitis & Linda Irwin-DeVitis
GENERAL EDITORS

As schools struggle to redefine and restructure themselves, they need to be cognizant of the new realities of adolescents. Thus, this series of monographs and textbooks is committed to depicting the variety of adolescent cultures that exist in today's post-industrial societies. It is intended to be a primarily qualitative research, practice, and policy series devoted to contextual interpretation and analysis that encompasses a broad range of interdisciplinary critique. In addition, this series will seek to provide a pragmatic, pro-active response to the current backlash of conservatism that continues to dominate political discourse, practice, and policy. This series seeks to address issues of curriculum theory and practice; multicultural education; aggression and violence; the media and arts; school dropouts; homeless and runaway youth; alienated youth; at-risk adolescent populations; family structures and parental involvement; and race, ethnicity, class, and gender studies.

Send proposals and manuscripts to the general editors at:
> Joseph L. DeVitis & Linda Irwin-DeVitis
> College of Education and Human Development
> University of Louisville
> Louisville, KY 40292-0001

To order other books in this series, please contact our Customer Service Department at:
> (800) 770-LANG (within the U.S.)
> (212) 647-7706 (outside the U.S.)
> (212) 647-7707 FAX

or browse online by series at:
> WWW.PETERLANGUSA.COM